Glamping

with
MaryJane

GLAMOUR + CAMPING

Glamping
with
MaryJane

MaryJane Butters

GIBBS SMITH
TO ENRICH AND INSPIRE HUMANKIND

First Edition
16 15 14 13 12   5 4 3 2 1

Published by
Gibbs Smith
P.O. Box 667
Layton, Utah 84041

1.800.835.4993 orders
www.gibbs-smith.com

Printed and bound in China

Gibbs Smith books are printed on either recycled, 100% post-consumer waste, FSC-certified papers or on paper produced from sustainable PEFC-certified forest/controlled wood source. Learn more at www.pefc.org.

ISBN: 978-1-4236-3081-4
Library of Congress Control Number: 2012937603

Art Direction by MaryJane Butters
Design by Alicia Baker and Carol Hill

Write to us at iris@maryjanesfarm.org or visit us on the Web at www.maryjanesfarm.org. MaryJane's personal blog can be found at www.raisingjane.org.

Dedicated to you,

and you and you and you

who ...

get it.

Author's Note

Why Glamour?

You know the scene. The happy '60s family pulls into a campsite. Father backs the trailer into position and unhitches it (or sets up a tent), hunts for firewood, starts a fire. Then, he finds a good spot for the family potty. His work done, he leaves to go fishing.

Mother entertains the children, fusses over the food, and gets the campsite ready. What she does next are the origins of the modern-day glamper. She drapes the table in an ironed tablecloth and proceeds to decorate it with a bouquet of just-picked wildflowers. Then she ties a pretty hankie on a lower tree branch by the potty, telling the kids to tie it high when they're behind the tree—hankie high, squatter's rights; hankie low, good-to-go.

Flash ahead 50 years to the next generation of campers, where the missus owns the trailer, backs it into position, unhitches it herself, and then goes fishing, but only after she's arranged all her special décor effects just so: a doily here, an ironing-board table there, a toity tent, and a pink barbeque grill ready for *her* catch of the day. Frilly this, and frilly that. It's a grown-up girl's version of playhouse. Pretend. Escape. Décor and more.

Between then and now, what's changed? Girl campers have ditched the notion that camping equipment is the domain of men (we're buying trailers as fast as we can find them); we've jettisoned the notion that going camping means you have to give up creature comforts like a billowy-soft bed, stamped linens, and bubble baths; we decorate our gypsy world (trailers and tents) in our favorite happy colors; we decal them (previously allowed only on home refrigerators); we hang our prom dresses right next to our lanterns; and we eat chocolate with abandon …

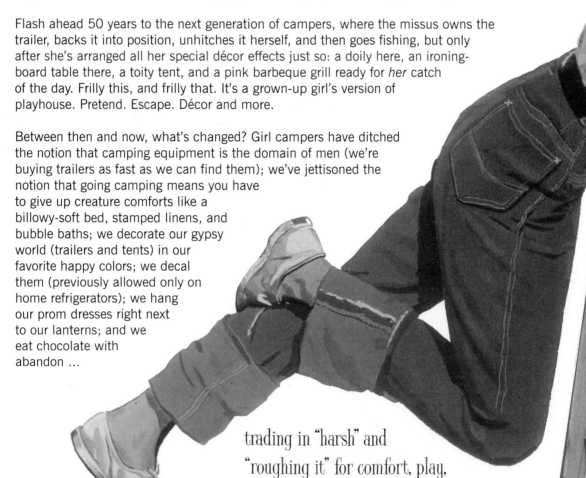

trading in "harsh" and
"roughing it" for comfort, play,
and style …

... 'nuff said?

> 66 Is that weird, taking my Louis Vuitton bag camping? 99
>
> – Jessica Simpson

Contents

trailer photos top right and bottom right courtesy of Suzanne Cummings

Introduction

Viewing Women's History
in 3-G
(Grit, Grace, and Glam)

The women who settled the West employed unadorned grit
(I'm talking the six-shooter variety), plenty of cast iron ("packing on pounds" back then meant hauling around your load of pots and pans), and canvas enough to push back the sky

—all of it ADORNED, of course, with a bit of glam—

a piece of torn white fabric worn as a neck or hair bow, a hollowed-out log made into a flower planter, a crocheted pull cord on a canvas tent flap, a tatted stampede hat string, a plain white flour sack turned into lace after 300 hours of punching needle holes at night—on the heels of punching calves all day.

"Glamping by glamplight," I call it ...

For this **IDAHO JANE**,

(former wilderness ranger turned organic farmer/author),

it was a bit of fun to have my unusual Idaho canvas wall-tent Bed & Breakfast featured in *National Geographic Traveler*, *Sunset*, *The New York Times Magazine*, and *Travel & Leisure,* to name a few (and even on the *Today Show* and the *Early Show*). *The New Yorker* magazine went so far as to write my life's story. In its predictable take on Westerners, the writer pointed out my tendency to drop Gs. More than happy to take their version of notoriety and run with it, I'm all about the three G's that really matter:

grit, grace, and glam.

I lived year-round in a wall tent in the Idaho outback

in the '70s while working for the Forest Service and have five wall tents presently set up at my farm outside Moscow, Idaho, for the purpose of offering an organic safari of sorts to those who want a chance to "unplug" and experience my version of camping,

or glamping, as I call it (one of those lost G's replacing the C in camping).

REMEMBER,
you were once wild,
you bathed in the
OPEN

My guests bathe and eat outdoors, sleep in tents that are gussied up with antique iron beds, billowy down comforters, frilly linens, and woodstoves.

When I was working on my first book in 2004, my New York City editors, in an unsuccessful effort to wall me in, insisted an Idaho "wall tent," as we've always called them, needed to be a "walled tent" in print in order to be proper. My reply?

"No ma'am, this is a wall tent; no pretenses out here, if you please, except for that pearl necklace strung around my lantern."

*Grandma camping w/daughters
(my mother and her sister)*

Wall tents back in my grandmother's day came octagonal, some even 12-sided, but mostly they were square and held up by two "gin poles."

I took my canvas (and gin pole) training when I worked for Emil Keck, an institution in Idaho's Selway-Bitterroot Wilderness.

My job description included growing a wilderness garden, remodeling an old log building, firefighting, some trail work, installing a new corral, taking care of pack animals, and after hours, some crochet. Before Keck's death in 1990, he was a living legend in the U.S. Forest Service. Irascible and unforgettable, he had an old-school work ethic that wouldn't quit … or take any flack from bureaucrats.

*Me, daughter Megan, and Emil Keck, 1981
I walked 27 miles with Meg on my back
so she could meet my former mentor, Emil Keck.*

His leadership, albeit harsh and cranky at times, inspired legions of forest workers as well as those who sought him out.

I lived year-round at the most remote ranger station in the lower forty-eight, surrounded only by canvas in a 14 x 16-foot wall tent. Once December hit, my tent was walled in by five feet of snow. (My job also entailed shoveling snow off the nearby historic ranger station.) But I stayed warm as long as I kept my fire banked. Because I cut my firewood by hand with an ax and a crosscut saw (no power tools allowed in the wilderness), I let it die out at night, which meant I awoke to a film of solid ice on my bedcovers, the result of taking in the sweetest, most virgin air Mother Nature has to offer—Idaho style. My wall-tent home was 27 miles from the end of a dirt road "up a might beyond Selway Falls, on past Three Links Bridge, stopping for a skinny dip at Maiden Creek, then onto … " by foot or on horse.

My mother, Helen Butters, 1925

1957

Me and brother Rex with catch of the day, 1961

Yippeeeee!!!
It's the Big Bonanza in
Musical Extravaganza!

Calamity
Jane

HOWARD
KEEL

DORIS
DAY

WARNER BROS.
SKY-HIGHEST
SMILE-WIDEST
WILD 'N' WOOLIEST
MUSICAL
OF 'EM ALL!

DVD

Like the infamous Calamity Jane who said,

"I figure if a girl wants to be a legend, she should go ahead and be one,"

I carved out my notoriety in the organic realm of things, serving as chair of Idaho's first official organic board back when organic was still a dirty word, long before the big chain stores would lay claim to anything organic. My self-sufficient Utah parents—who took us camping every weekend—raised me exclusively on the organic food they'd grown themselves, so it was only "natural" I'd end up with sales of a million dollars per year in organic backpacking food—The Simple Life, Inc.

Pregnant with my first child and intentionally homeless except for the 14-foot travel trailer shown here peeking out from behind where I posed for a photograph with my friend Sara,

I spent months four and five of my pregnancy on the road behind the wheel of my '53 pickup truck (the same vintage as I am), pulling a two-toned pink and yellow-trimmed, grown-up dollhouse named "Wildflower."

Those two months were to be the last of my full-time "tramping" (trailer camping) days—I've been rooted ever since. By the time my daughter, Meg, was born, I had moved onto a ranch and into a house in White Bird, Idaho.

"Wildflower" was a beauty, inside and out.

Her previous owners were my parents, so she was a familiar companion to me, and I've often wondered if I'll bump into her again somewhere, somehow.

Her interior was a study in the utilization of space.

Everything had its designated place.

Her charming interior was mostly wood with pine veneer cabinets and very little plastic, although music in that era was still plenty vinyl, the likes of which John Prine sang "Pink Cadillac" and Nanci Griffith sang "Montana Backroads" to me whenever I could find a plug-in for my portable record player.

My mother had kept Wildflower clean as a whistle, and I learned how to make her floors and counters shine. When she wasn't on the road for family outings in the late '60s, she became an oversized "playhouse" for me and my gaggle of girlfriends.

I've never gotten over my love of small spaces, where everything has its place and every square inch serves a purpose. When I'm out and about and I see a trailer coming, I wonder if, maybe this time, it'll be her! I do miss her gleaming skin, her hand-crank windows, her ovoid profile, and her unapologetic Spartan style.

Trailer for sale or rent ... Queen of the Road!

66 When the

whole world is
your living room,
a tiny house seems plenty. 99

– Jay Shafer, Tumbleweed Tiny House Company

The "bringing back good food" part of my journey (every Idaho farmer was an organic farmer 70 years ago) has been a long, hard pull for me, but bringing back the glamping part of Idaho's her-story has been as easy as having my son paint my biodiesel Mercedes-Benz pink to match my fingernails and then hitching up my glamper (vintage-style teardrop trailer) and heading to the hills. (I also have a classic Airstream and Shasta that I pull with my farm truck.)

In other words, women GET IT, big time.

The very minute you show up or drive by pulling a "glamper" or they see one of my wall tents "all girled up," they get out their doilies, fishing poles, and chipped enamel pots. It's in our blood.

It's part of our her-itage.

Joining our ranks is easy enough.

I'm here to walk you through it step-by-step, side-by-side, detail-by-detail ...

Trailers

... I did say detail, didn't I?
Le toilet "details" on page 76.

IN THIS CHAPTER

Trailer Shopping & Restoration

Lucy fan? Here's a movie that will get you in trailer mode.

(Re)Search & Rescue

Airstream, Shasta, Spartan, the coveted Covered Wagon ... there are so many makes and models and manufacturers. How do you choose?

Google it, girlfriend.

When it comes to starting the hunt for that new-to-you trailer, research is your best friend. There are hundreds of websites devoted to these little darlings, and the vintage trailer crowd is a generous, friendly sort who love to share their stories, insights, and suggestions.

Visit my website, InternationalGlampingWeekend.com, for a list of helpful and informative websites and blogs, or start Googlin' and see what comes up. Before you know it, you'll have the lay of the land.

A few things to consider:

Size matters
Will you be a solo glamper gal, or are you packin' a family along with you? A 15-foot trailer will usually sleep four, but it'll be tight. Also check out 18-foot and 20-foot trailers to find the one that fits.

Comfort counts too
Camping always involves a little bit of roughing it, but you *are* a glampin' girl after all—so decide how much comfort you want. Shower? Toilet? Air-conditioning? Heat?

Do the math
Once you've cutie-spied your dream trailer, you're going to want to take it everywhere. What do you have to pull it with? Find out the towing capacity/weight limit of your vehicle (check the owner's manual or call your dealer), and keep in mind that this will need to include passengers as well. You don't want to have to buy a new car just to tow your little trailer around (... or do you?).

Towing capacity
A factory-installed towing package will mean you can pull your weight and then some, but if you chose to forego that option when you purchased your vehicle, you can still get your glamp on by having a towing package installed after the fact. BUT, and this is a big but, you have to match all the pieces. If everything in your system is beefy but the tow ball, your entire towing system (tongue, hitch, etc.) will "dumb down" to its weakest link. See p. 42 for more about getting hitched.

Stick to Your Budget

Trailers come in all kinds of conditions, with all kinds of price tags. A smart glamper gal is savvy, not spendy, and key to this is knowing what you want to spend before you even start looking.

Prices of vintage trailers are based on many factors, including age, condition, size, original or unique features, and popularity. They range from $500 to $5,000 for a fixer-upper, or a little (or a lot!) more for something partially or fully restored ... make sure your pick matches your pocketbook.

Vintage trailers are often project purchases—elbow grease is absolutely part of the trampin' glamper's lifestyle. Unless you have the means to purchase a fully restored trailer, which might mean spending 10 to 15 thou' or more, you'll want to factor in fixes, restorations, and improvements into your budget.

Strippin' it down and starting over is a big job, but lots of people do it. You can do it, too. And every glamper girl already knows that a smaller budget doesn't have to mean scrimping on style.

Buyer Beware

Although online shopping is definitely the way to go when it comes to searching for your new glamping home on wheels, repeat after me ... never, ever, ever buy a vintage trailer sight unseen. Ever.

Well, at least not usually. A lovingly (and adorably) restored trailer, like the one pictured here that I found on The Loyal Order of the Glamper's Facebook page, is a good example of one I might feel comfortable buying without physical inspection. A husband and wife team, they remake trailers as a hobby, and they explained everything to me in detail over the phone. Cute!

Potential Budget Busters:

Improvement and restoration costs are up to you, but you should be able to negotiate the estimated costs of any repairs, especially essential mechanical repairs, from the purchase price.

And please remember that falling in love with a vintage trailer is akin to falling in love. It happens. But you mustn't let infatuation inflate what is. You have to know what you want and stick to it.

Sigh ... you know how it goes, girls. Certain fellas think a woman is a walking target, and suddenly the price goes up. The best defense is to be informed. Make sure that when he starts to talk axles and propane systems, you can talk 'em right back. Knowing your stuff will put that rascally hustler in his place. Of course, a bit of fiercely feminine glamporific gumption never hurts either.

For Sale: Shasta Compact located in WA. $5,500. Has a pink stove!

Adorable exceptions aside, getting to know your potential purchase up close and personal is the only way to ensure you know *exactly* what you're getting into. You don't want to come down with a bad case of buyer's remorse.

Pictures may be worth a thousand words, but they may not be worth thousands of dollars.

1962 Shasta 14' (Wings) - $2800

Date: 2012-04-09, 6:11PM PDT

Very well preserved original Shasta with wings. No disappointments! Hard to find rear kitchen. The exterior is aluminum and the bottom of the sides are aqua. This trailer has been restored as necessary. Recent trip from Tahoe to Washington, perfect run with no problems. Good trailer for vintage rallys.

3 ways to tell a Fib

cheap caulkins
mold
water damage
holes

Let me be your example of why sight-unseen can be a problem. If you're like me, you're an optimist. You hope for the best. Plus, you're short on time. When I talked to the owner of this Shasta (that I ended up buying sight-unseen for $2,500), he said there wasn't any mold or water damage. (I asked twice.) And all the windows and outside lights had been recaulked. But he failed to mention a cheap caulk had been used that you can scrape off with your fingernail. Oh, and there was definitely mold and water damage. In addition, he didn't mention the gaping holes in the side or rust in the fridge or the fact that the stove didn't work OR that it had a shady history and had been stolen in a former life (revealed during the title transfer). When my farmhand pulled it into my driveway after a five-hour drive, I wrote the seller an e-mail expressing my dismay. To his credit, he said, "I would be happy to take it back and pay for the gas for the return trip." Once I got the windows washed, I could see her potential. So I kept her, but I will never buy a trailer again without seeing it first.

Before you hand over your hard-earned cash, you have some serious investigatin' to do. To that end, allow me to introduce you to …

The Four W's of Vintage Trailer Shopping

① What to Ask & Ask & Ask (a Glampin' Gal's Triple A)

Everything! Ask everything. Then ask again. Don't be afraid to ask all the questions you can think of, and make sure you get clear answers. When was the trailer last used and by whom? (This one's important because a trailer used for hunting trips or other manly-type excursions is almost always a bit trashed and smelly). When were the brakes last checked? New tires? Any leaks? Any mold? Any mice? Any major mechanical issues? Or structural issues? Is the title clear? A trustworthy seller will have nothing to hide and should be happy to answer ALL your questions.

② What to Look For

You've asked all your questions, now it's time to take matters into your own hands. A thorough inspection will take some time, so don't rush—and don't let yourself be rushed by an overly eager seller.

Water Damage

The most costly repair will be water damage. Unfortunately, vintage trailers are notoriously leaky or they can have damage from inside condensation. There could be varying degrees of water damage—stains aren't easy to fix if you want to keep the original wood, and rotting inside the framing is a major rebuild. Leaking can also soften and rot the floor, which is a major fix. And then there's mold. Besides the ewwwh factor, mold can be dangerous, smelly, and difficult to kill. Check all the windows, vents, and seams for signs of leaking or water damage.

Tip: A fresh coat of paint can be a good thing—unless it's covering up water damage. Look closely!

Follow Your Nose

An old trailer is bound to smell a bit musty, but a stronger, unpleasant smell can be a bigger problem. Mice love to move into the walls of unused trailers and nest there. Cleaning up their mess can mean tearing apart the interior structure (see p. 35). If the infestation was major, the smell can be nearly impossible to get rid of. Cushions can also be culprits when it comes to holding onto bad smells, which could mean more money if your plans to glamp-up the trailer involved recovering instead of replacing.

Tip: If you can smell it, find it. Identify all bad smells and evaluate the damage.

Get Turned On

When it comes to the electrical system, there are three words you need to remember: Plug. It. In. If a seller isn't willing to show you that the electrical system works or tells you the lights that run off a battery can't be tested because the battery is dead, it probably means they don't work. Repairs are doable, but it may mean taking down interior walls and paying for a complete rewiring.

Tip: Most vintage trailers will have two electrical systems: one for the interior power outlets, and one for the brake lights, turn signals, etc. Check both.

Appliances & Plumbing

Vintage trailer appliances usually run on propane, and a broken propane line can be dangerous. Have the seller show you that the propane and plumbing systems work. Again, this will require hooking things up, which a cooperative seller should be happy to do. Turn on the faucets, flush the toilet (if there is one), light the stove, etc.

Tip: Know your state laws and safety regulations for propane use, and ask the seller if a recent propane pressure test has been done.

Get Down

A true glampin' gal isn't afraid to get a little grease on her hands or a little dust on her denim. When you're trailer shopping, inspecting your potential purchase means checking it out from all sides, including underneath. An unexpected broken or cracked axle can be a big expense—and a big bummer if it breaks as you're gallivantin' to your very first glampout. Also check the tires. Just like that ex-boyfriend, they tend to get bald spots.

> **Tip:** If the current tires seem in good shape, ask the seller when the bearings were last packed. If you will be replacing the tires, make sure to get ones made specifically for an RV or travel trailer.

A Hitch in Your Plans

Hitches aren't nearly as complicated and scary as they look, and my "Gettin' Hitched" section on p. 42 gives complete instructions on how to get things properly hooked up. As you evaluate a trailer, you should make sure the hitch is in good shape, the safety chains (there should be two) are in place and solid, and take note of the tow wiring. It will likely take some rewiring to hook up your vintage trailer to your modern car, but a mechanic should be able to handle this easily.

> **Tip:** Speaking of mechanics ... know one? See p. 136. Bring him with you when you do your inspecting. (Bring a fresh box of donuts along for bribery ... I mean, incentive).

③ What to Bring (Inspecting Gadgets)

Every girl needs a tool kit (see p. 119). Period. But you'll need a few specific things to help you inspect your potential new trailer. In addition to the flashlight and 4-in-1 screwdriver you have in your tool kit, gather up these extra items before you head out:

- **Heavy-duty Extension Cord**—In case the seller doesn't have one, you'll want to be able to plug in the trailer to test the electricity.
- **Electrical 3-prong Adapter**—A handy thing to have anyway, just to be sure you can plug everything in.
- **Electrical Tester**—A cool little device that will let you easily test the outlets inside the trailer. (If you don't have this, ask the seller to plug in an old lamp or cell phone.)
- **Water Hose**—Might be cumbersome to keep in your car, but you don't want the seller to have any excuse not to test the water system for you. It's a good idea to have some extra connectors and couplings as well. As you test the system, look for any leaks on the ground underneath the trailer. Note: A garden hose will probably work for testing purposes, but for use during camping you will need to buy a water hose that is FDA or NSF approved for drinking water (available at any RV supply store).
- **Rubber Gloves**—Dirt under your fingernails is one thing; mouse droppings are another.
- **Barbeque Lighter**—Provided there's some propane in the tank, you'll need a lighter to test the oven and stove.

> **Tip:** For formulating future decorating plans, a tape measure and some paint chips or fabric swatches might be handy.

④ When to Walk Away (Those Boots Were Made for ...)

I know. It hurts. You found the most adorable little trailer and every night you were falling asleep to sweet, glittering glamping dreams—but her wiring is bad, her floor is caving in, her walls are moldy, and no amount of perfume (or bleach) could get rid of her dreadful smell. You have to let her go. You were born to be a glamper; you'll find another.

Anything that makes you uncomfortable is reason to walk away. Extensive rodent or water damage, a rotted exterior with too many rusty holes, out-of-control mold, or too many sloppy repairs that will have to be redone are all potential reasons to move on.

More Vintage Trailer Shopping Tips

Acquire Some Skills
Attend a workshop on buying a vintage trailer like the one at right, offered by the Starlite Classic Campground.

Make Some Connections
Attend a Vintage Trailer Rally. Stroll around and talk to folks. Ask them for suggestions and advice. Ask to take a peek inside their trailers (they love to show off their darlings!). For a list of rallies, see my website, InternationalGlampingWeekend.com.

Be Social (Media)
Find vintage trailer or glamping groups on Facebook or Pinterest. Or start your own.

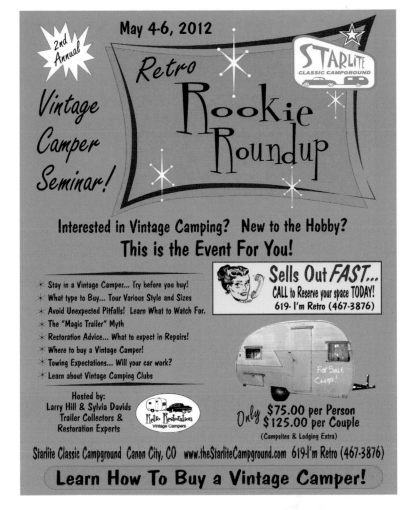

May 4-6, 2012

2nd Annual

Vintage Camper Seminar!

STARLITE CLASSIC CAMPGROUND

Retro Rookie Roundup

Interested in Vintage Camping? New to the Hobby?
This is the Event For You!

* Stay in a Vintage Camper... Try before you buy!
* What type to Buy... Tour Various Style and Sizes
* Avoid Unexpected Pitfalls! Learn What to Watch For.
* The "Magic Trailer" Myth
* Restoration Advice... What to expect in Repairs!
* Where to buy a Vintage Camper!
* Towing Expectations... Will your car work?
* Learn about Vintage Camping Clubs

Sells Out FAST...
CALL to Reserve your space TODAY!
619- I'm Retro (467-3876)

For Sale Cheap!

Hosted by:
Larry Hill & Sylvia Davids
Trailer Collectors &
Restoration Experts

Retro Restoration Vintage Campers

Only **$75.00 per Person**
$125.00 per Couple
(Campsites & Lodging Extra)

Starlite Classic Campground Canon City, CO www.theStarliteCampground.com 619-I'm Retro (467-3876)

Learn How To Buy a Vintage Camper!

Taking It to the Streets

Be sure to keep it legal. Ask the seller for the title and make sure it is clear. If the title has been lost, which is likely with a vintage trailer, you'll have to request a new one. The process for titling and registration of a trailer is much the same as for a car, but check with your DMV, as the requirements differ from state to state.

What Else to Look For
Vintage trailers are full of vintage furnishings. They may need some TLC or rewiring, but original fixtures can add loads of charm to your trailer. And if they absolutely don't fit your style, you can always sell them to someone who wants them for her trailer. So while you're checking things out, see what can be salvaged.

Tip: If you've done your research beforehand, you'll have a good idea of any special features the trailer might've originally had, and you'll have a better idea of what to look for.

Not-So-Do-It-Yourself Diva
Vintage trailer restoration is big business, and there are plenty of professionals who will take your trailer from forgotten to fabulous for you. Ask around for recommendations, and find listings on my website, InternationalGlampingWeekend.com.

In-Over-My-Head Airstream Restoration

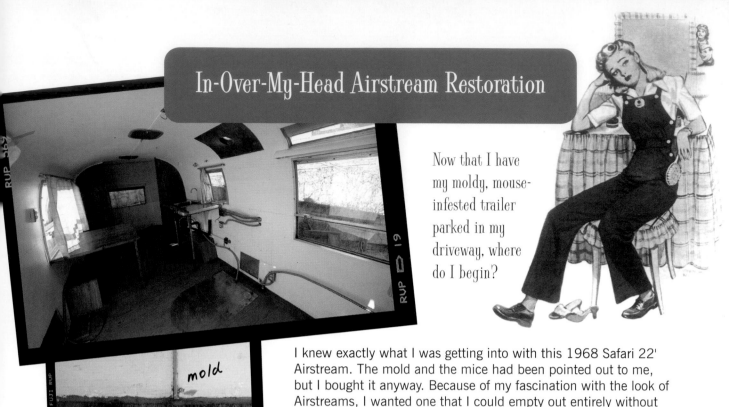

Now that I have my moldy, mouse-infested trailer parked in my driveway, where do I begin?

mold

mice

walls coming down

I knew exactly what I was getting into with this 1968 Safari 22' Airstream. The mold and the mice had been pointed out to me, but I bought it anyway. Because of my fascination with the look of Airstreams, I wanted one that I could empty out entirely without feeling guilty. This had been a bachelor pad, so all of the original Airstream fixtures—sink, toilet, cabinets, etc.—were already gone. It was perfect for me, because I wanted a tiny house and not so much a travel trailer. When I'm on the road, I like the travel ease of my teardrop.

First, a window rebuild (VintageTrailerSupply.com for gaskets), in addition to butyl caulking around all the fixed windows. Then, the painted inside aluminum walls came down by drilling out all the rivets that held them up. (I only put one of the huge, heavy fiberglass ends back in when I put the walls back up, so the front end required strips of contoured plywood riveted in place.) The next step was the most daunting and disgusting. There was an entire mouse CITY in the fiberglass insulation in the walls. Everything was cleaned thoroughly with alcohol. Good riddance. (I hate mieces to pieces.)

Then, any holes where the mice and water were coming in needed to be mended. A combination of foil-faced rigid and foil-faced bubble insulation came next. Then, electrical, Internet, and TV wiring (all new and old wires were threaded through plastic chases when going through the structural aluminum). Several cans of foam later, and she was tight as a drum. The aluminum walls went back up using new rivets. Decorative thermoplastic panels from ACPIdeas.com were glued in place (girly frill). Appliances, cabinets, and stove next came next. I purchased my propane fridge and stovetop at VintageTrailerSupply.com. Did you know a propane fridge is silent? (Hasn't it been said that women prefer the silent type?) I also researched and found, I think, the only on-demand propane hot-water heater that would fill my 4½' vintage claw-foot bathtub quickly. And then … typical of construction projects, my book came due and I'd run out of time. My tell-all trailer wasn't totally glammed out yet. What's a girl to do? Onto plan B …

I know it doesn't look glamorous now, but ...

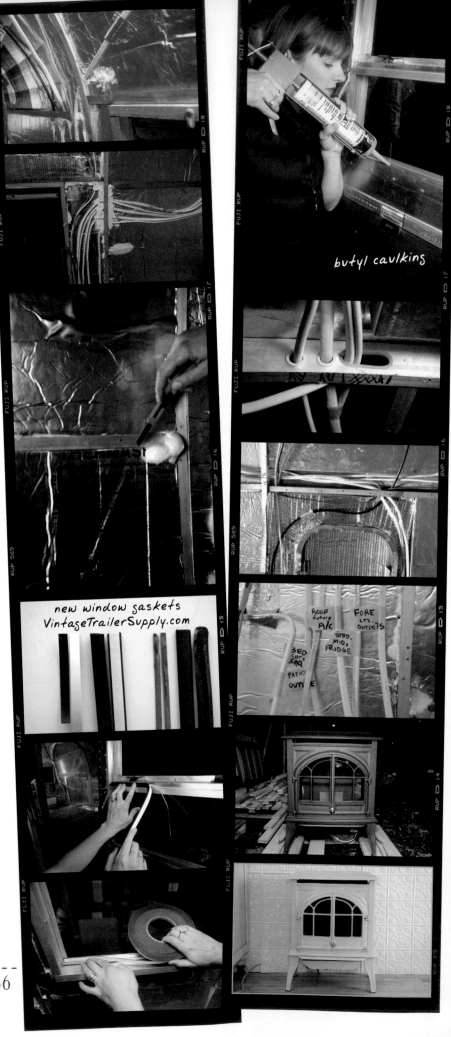

new window gaskets
VintageTrailerSupply.com

butyl caulkins

fresh new rivets

hardwood floor repurposed
from a basketball court

plastic
fake
tin
ceiling

It's almost there! You'll see my dream glamper, brought back to life, along with how-to details, on my International Glamping Weekend website, internationalglampingweekend.com.

fridge

future home of clawfoot tub

built-in bed here

Adorning "Girlfriend"

Paint, Decals, Signage

Time to gussy-up, girls! You want your vintage trailer to make her glamping debut looking finer than ever, and that will probably mean some fresh paint.

Any window and hardware replacements and all caulking should be done before you paint. Proper prep is paramount, and that means a good washing with lots of soapy water. For an older trailer especially, use a mildly abrasive scouring pad to remove any oxidized or chalking paint. You'll also need to sand out any rust spots.

Let's say you've decided on a Rosie the Riveter theme for your trailer. And why not? Rosie is strong and glamorous—just like you. There are three ways to get your Rosie on: paint, decals, or metal signage.

See how to make a dish-drainer quilt on p. 95

Sixth Street Gallery, Prosser, WA

A coat of chalkboard paint on the inside of your glamper door is a good way to issue an invitation to your glamping buddies. Opened up, it's a message board.

QUANTITY BURGOO STEW

About 70 squirrels, cut up
2 large stewing chickens, cut up
6 gal. water
2½ lb. salt pork, chopped
2½ gal. butter beans
3½ gal. cubed potatoes
4 gal. chopped, peeled tomatoes
1 gal. cubed carrots
2½ gal. freshly cut corn
1 gal. shredded cabbage
1 pod red pepper, chopped
¾ c. black pepper
1¾ c. salt
1 lb. sugar

Much like the clambake of today, burgoo stew was a favorite with folks in the South in the early '40s. Farm families put a big iron kettle over a bed of coals and everyone brought an ingredient.

Burgoo Stew HERE 6:00pm Sharp!!

Let's talk 'em through:

Paint

You'll need to know if your trailer is fiberglass, aluminum, or metal, and choose your paint accordingly. Be sure to use exterior paint, whether it's latex or oil-based. Have fun with your colors—and remember gloss is best to give your glamper that happy glow.

It's a good idea to apply a coat of primer to your clean and sanded trailer and let it dry for several hours before you begin painting.

Once the primer is dry, wipe the trailer down again to remove any dust, and use painter's tape (retire your masking tape) to cover up any chrome or trim, and also to mark any stripes or designs you want for the body of the trailer. You can also find automotive paint pens for freehanding any lettering or designs—including Rosie. This might also be the time to call upon your most fanciful artist friends to help you paint a mural or landscape using small brushes, bright colors, and lots of creativity.

Apply the paint with rollers and thick brushes, or rent a sprayer. If you go with spraying, you'll need a garage or other inside space where paint won't be swept away with the breeze. And this is IMPORTANT—you'll also need a painter's respirator. If using rollers, buy them in varying lengths, or cut larger ones to different sizes, to give you more versatility with your painting.

Decals

Sooo easy. Simply take the image you want to your local sign shop and tell them you want it as a vehicle graphic. They'll print it on a vinyl decal that can easily be applied to your trailer.

Be sure the area where you want your decal is clean and dry. You may want to wipe it down with alcohol to remove any wax because vinyl will not adhere well to any wax or coating.

If you don't have access to a sign shop, websites like StickViews.com are a fun way to create and order custom (and affordable!) car decals.

Metal Signage

You saw the most adorable metal Rosie the Riveter sign at your local antique mall and it was love at first sight. Once your trailer is cleaned and painted, grab your drill and rivets (they must be the rust-proof variety) and rivet Rosie right onto your trailer, paying attention to where electrical and plumbing lines might be. My preference for attaching metal to metal is to use stainless-steel metal screws with a spot of butyl rubber pushed into the hole you drilled to receive the screws, sealing it from moisture as you seat the screw.

Gettin' Hitched

Well, now, would you look at Jane!

With her trailer fine-tuned and fancied-up, she's finally ready to roam. She'll be heading down the highway in no time, on the move, freewheeling with the wind.

But first, she needs to get hitched.

It's not what it sounds like, trust me.

Jane needs to hitch her wagon to a … car.

In order to get rolling, Jane needs to fasten "Freedom" (every trailer needs a name) to the rig that will carry them both down the road.

Our glamperific gal sashays over to her jaunty li'l Jeep, boots clomping and skirts swinging. With a tip of her hat, she hops behind the wheel and puts 'er in reverse. She sees the trailer in her rearview. Check. Everything looks pretty straight. No worries. Just back that tow ball up to the trailer hitch.

This isn't so hard, right? CRUNCH.

Uh-oh …

Been there? Done that? Rest assured, it's happened to the best of us.

Let's just make sure it doesn't happen again.

Basic Towing Talk

Trailer hitch: the towing device that's mounted to your vehicle and connects it to the trailer.

Note: Hitch ball mounts come in different sizes depending on the height of your vehicle. Below is a 8" drop, at left is a zero drop.

Trailer tongue: the long part of the trailer base that sticks out forward and attaches to the vehicle's trailer hitch.

Hitch ball: the ball-shaped attachment on the trailer hitch. **Trailer coupler:** the part of the trailer tongue that cups the hitch ball and secures the trailer to your vehicle.

Coupler latching mechanism: a latch on top of the coupler that "locks" the coupler to the hitch ball. (This is what a girlfriend of mine forgot to do and her trailer came loose.)

Coupler Lock: ensures that the coupler latching mechanism can't accidentally lift up.

Tongue jack: a jack mechanism mounted to the trailer tongue, allowing the front of the trailer to be raised and lowered to match up to the hitch.

Safety chains: chains attached to the trailer tongue with hooks on their free ends.

Electrical Hook-up: synchronizes your trailers' lights and signals with your vehicle.

Chances are, you won't need a big ole truck to pull your cute li'l glamp trailer. In fact, just about any vehicle with a measure of muscle will do the job.

Top 2 things to know before you tow:

① Trailer Weight

Your trailer's weight will be listed on a sticker somewhere on the trailer (it's required by law). Check inside the cabinets and near the tongue. The actual towed weight of your trailer is called the UVW (Unloaded Vehicle Weight). It doesn't include updates you've made to the trailer (like the vintage claw-foot tub in my Airstream) or accessories installed by a dealer, so you'll need to factor in those additions plus the anticipated weight of the cargo you plan to carry. The manufacturer-recommended weight limit for the trailer will also be listed on the sticker. Look for GTW (Gross Trailer Weight).

② Vehicle Towing Capacity

To find out how much weight your vehicle can safely tow, check your vehicle's owner's manual or call a car dealer and ask.

When it comes to towing and weight, U-Haul is a one-stop shop. Those folks are hip to all things hitch-related, and they can offer important tips for successful towing.

Run by your local U-Haul dealer to get the lowdown on your current hitch capacity, or let them equip your vehicle with the setup that's best suited to your trailer.

You'll also find all sorts of helpful info at UHaul.com.

Hitchin' Up

Backing a vehicle up to a trailer is something that looks incredibly easy. Mind you, I said *looks*. Watching somebody (such as handsome, handy hubby) back up to a hitch is inspiring. How hard can it be?

Once you're in the driver's seat, it's a different story. Most of your maneuvering is based on mirrors, and mirrors offer a pretty limited view of the world beyond the rear bumper.

Practice (and patience) will almost certainly make perfect over time, but who has time? And while a helper can make all the difference, sometimes having "help" is more frustrating than it's worth. (I have always preferred to make my mistakes in private.)

So, here's a bit of gladsome news for the independent glamper: I discovered a magic mirror—yes, the fairest of them all—that reveals exactly what you need to see in order to hitch up in a hurry:

- The Hitch Ball Finder (about $25 at CampingWorld.com) is a convex mirror that mounts with magnets on a telescoping pole to show you the hitch ball and trailer coupler.

The men in your life will never know how you did it without their help.

Practice tip: Rent a small U-Haul trailer (with insurance), and practice hooking up. We don't want Jane busting up her beautified baby trailer now, do we?

Once you've backed into place, follow these simple steps to make sure your trailer hooks up safe and sound:

1 Make sure the latching mechanism is pulled up and the coupler is lined up over the hitch ball.

2 Crank the handle on the trailer's tongue jack to lower the coupler down onto the ball. If the coupler doesn't fall easily onto the ball and the jack is raised fully, you may need to hop up on the trailer tongue and give a little bounce to force the coupler down firmly onto the ball. (Make sure your latching mechanism is fully open. Jiggle and wiggle it if not.)

3 Push the coupler latching mechanism down and secure it with the coupler lock. Retract the tongue jack all the way up. (Remove the wheel if your model of tongue jack has one. Some wheels are permanently attached, but some don't have a wheel and the tongue jack must be lowered onto a block of wood.)

4 Attach the safety chains on your trailer hitch to your vehicle, leaving some slack. Should the trailer break away from the hitch, the chains will keep it attached to your vehicle.

5 Plug your trailer's electrical connection into your vehicle's receptor. This controls your trailer's taillights, brake lights, turn signals, and side marker lights. Some newer trailers have connectors that also control the trailer's braking system.

6 Final checks include making sure the trailer's lights and signals are synchronized with your vehicle. Check all of your connections again to make sure you're hooked up securely.

You're good to go!

Beep, Beep—Back It Up, Girlfriend

Remember that U-Haul trailer you rented to practice hitching up? Don't return it just yet.

Now that you're a pro at hooking up, tow your U-Haul to a big, empty parking lot with well-marked spaces, and practice backing it into a space. Practice, practice, and practice some more. You *will* get the hang of it, I promise. At first, it helps to have a lot of space to move around in and no audience to fluster you.

Here's how you do it:

1. Place your left hand on the bottom of the steering wheel. Turn your body to the right and watch your trailer through the back window of your vehicle.
2. As you back up, move your steering hand in the direction you want the trailer to go.
3. Don't turn too tightly and "jackknife" the trailer (stuck in a 90-degree position that can damage your vehicle or trailer). Stop and pull forward as many times as necessary to get out of a jackknife when it happens. Not if. When. It will happen. Most importantly, try not to feel pressured. It's not a race—better to back in safe than sorry.

Once you're feeling more confident on your own, don't shy away from help.

A helper standing outside the vehicle can make the process of slipping into a tight spot a lot easier.
(But like I said, I prefer making my mistakes in private.)

Playing with a kid's toy truck and trailer helps, too. Vrrrm, Vrrrm.

My trailer may be wee, but my welcome is big.

This book will be at the printer about the time our 2012 first annual International Glamping Weekend takes place. We're planning something even more grand for 2013, June 1 & 2. Check our website for details, InternationalGlampingWeekend.com. Please join us in 2013. We'll keep our lamp lit and our tent flap open.

Drive It

- When loading your glamping gear, make sure your load is balanced, with about 60% of the total weight in front. Balance the weight from side to side as well.
- On the road, allow plenty of stopping and following distance between you and other vehicles. It takes a lot longer to stop a trailer than a car alone.
- Change lanes carefully, using your mirrors to make sure there is plenty of room in the lane you want to enter.
- Avoid passing other cars unless you have to, especially on two-lane roads. (Actually, I have a friend who is an EMT and he says NEVER, under any circumstances, pass anyone. Period.)
- Be courteous to faster traffic, using turnouts whenever possible and staying in the slower lane.
- Don't pull into a place where you can't see an exit because it's easy to get stuck with a trailer. Look for parking that has easy access, in and out.

Park It

After you back into a campsite or parking space, it's time to chock, level, and lock—the easiest campsite setup you've ever seen.

1 Time to chock your wheels. Even on level surfaces, place wheel chocks (CampingWorld.com) in front of and behind your trailer's tires to make sure it doesn't roll. Kick each chock toward the tire to secure it.

2 In order to unhitch, lower your "landing gear" (the trailer's tongue jack) onto a block of wood or wheel if it has one. Lift the coupler lock and remove the safety chains.

3 Raise the height of the jack until the coupler lifts off the hitch ball. Pull your vehicle forward, out from under the coupler. Adjust the height of the tongue jack until the trailer looks level from front-to-back.

4 Place bottle, scissor jacks, or interlocking plastic leveling blocks (CampingWorld.com) to get ready to level the trailer and secure it. Perfectly level isn't necessary, but the closer you get, the more comfortable you'll be inside your trailer.

5 Check how level your trailer is from front-to-back. You can eyeball it, but it's more accurate to use a carpenter's level.

6 Now check how level your trailer is from side-to-side. You can put your carpenter's level on the floor of the trailer or an outside window sill. (Get clever and mount a small level permanently on a side window and one on the front or back window.)

7 Use a wheel lock (ETrailer.com) when parked so that no one can hook up your trailer and haul it away. (ETrailer.com is a good resource for more details on all of the above.)

Insurance

Just the Facts, Ma'am

- Your travel trailer must be registered with your state vehicle licensing department.
- Travel trailers and campers do not require special highway permits for towing.
- You are not legally required to purchase insurance for your travel trailer.

Famous Last Words:

"If trailer insurance isn't required by law, then forget it."
(Insert cautionary head-shaking and tongue-clucking here.)

Just because trailer insurance isn't legally mandated, doesn't mean it's not a critical consideration.

Your trailer may be covered under your vehicle's liability insurance policy (check with your insurance company), but there are other aspects of coverage to contemplate. Theft, vandalism, collision—you know the drill. When you're traveling "out there" on America's highways and byways, you'll feel more carefree if you're safe, sister, not sorry.

Shop for Insurance

As with home and auto insurance, shop around to find the best deal on trailer coverage.

- Start with your car insurance company and ask about package rates for multiple policies.
- Search other auto insurance companies for comparison.
- Get a free online quote at RVAInsurance.com.

Request a Quote

When requesting an insurance quote, have the following info on hand:

- Type of trailer (teardrop, pop-up, etc.)
- Trailer length and width
- Purchase price
- Make, model, and serial number

Explore Options

Trailer insurance can be as basic or as comprehensive as you choose. Consider the following coverages as you shop for your perfect policy:

Liability

Covers physical injury and property damage caused to others in an accident.

Total Loss Replacement

Fully replaces your trailer if destroyed (usually within the first 5 model years), or pays you the original purchase price of your trailer.

Roadside Assistance

Provides 24/7 help in the event of an emergency, including towing, locksmith services, tire repair, and getting your trailer unstuck from snow, mud, etc.

Accessories

Covers the "doo-dads" on your trailer, such as awnings, antennas, shutters, bling, and so on.

Emergency Expenses

Helps pay for hotel stays and car rentals if you're involved in an accident far from home.

Fire, Flood, and Theft

Covers your trailer and contents in the event of unforeseen disasters.

Collision

Covers damages from an accident with another vehicle.
May also cover personal items inside your trailer.

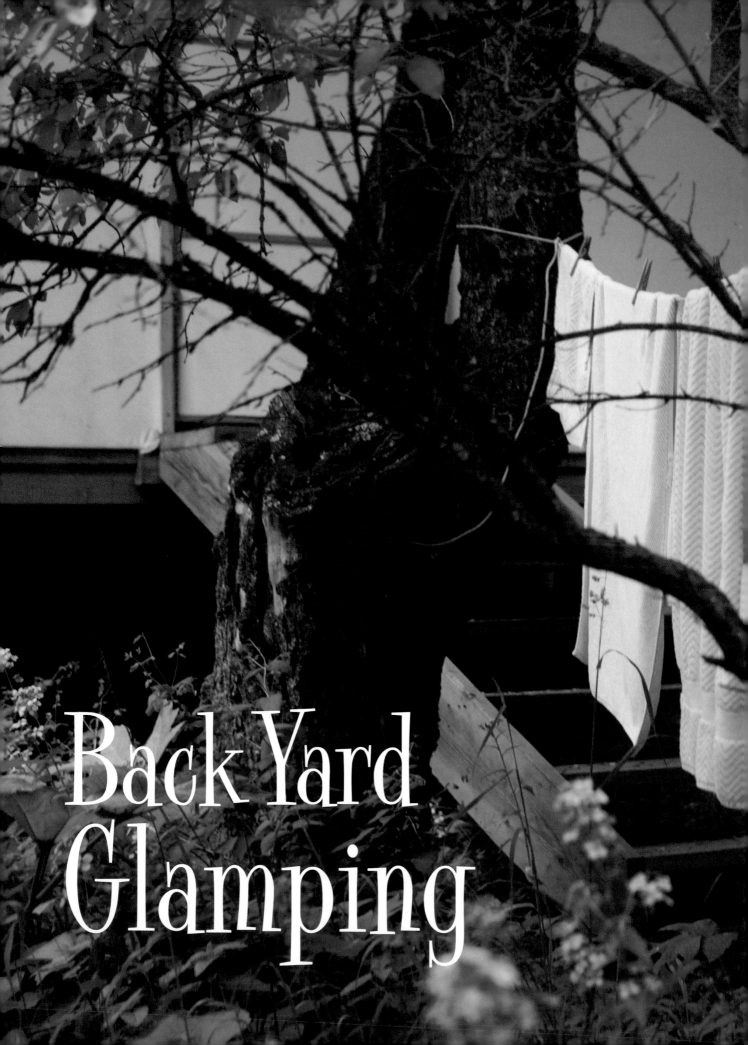

Back Yard
Glamping

" ... once alone, it is impossible to believe that one could ever have been otherwise. Loneliness is an absolute **"** discovery.

– Marilynne Robinson,
Housekeeping

IN THIS CHAPTER

DIY Canvas Cabin Retreat

Make a Wall Tent of Your Own

More than a tent, not quite a cabin, a wall tent is a canvas tent that is stretched over a wooden frame and a raised floor. If you buy a piece of farm ground, this is a great way to stay on the property while you build a house.

My tent platform job took 12 hours total from start to finish, and the materials cost about $750. Because some of the wooden boards you'll be buying are longer than what you can easily haul in a pickup truck, I recommend that you make other arrangements for delivery. Most building-supply yards offer a delivery service for a reasonable fee.

These plans fit the 12' x 14' wall tents I purchased from Colorado Yurt Company (ColoradoYurt.com), but you can purchase premade tents to top your frame in a number of sizes; or from other manufacturers; just adjust the dimensions of the frame accordingly.

Tent Frame Supply List

For a 12' x 14' wall tent, you'll need:

8	12" x 12"	concrete pier blocks
4	4x6 x 16'	beams
7	2x6 x 20'	floor joists
40	2x6 x 12'	decking boards
5	2x4 x 12'	guy line rail supports and bracing
2	2x4 x 16'	guy line rails
4	pounds	16-penny galvanized nails
3	pounds	3" deck screws
40	2"	plated wood screws with fender washers (to attach the lower side walls of the tent to the outer edges of the deck along the 14' length)

- Additional 2x4 and/or 4x4 pieces may be required for columns and to brace the 4x6 beams, depending upon how level the ground is at the platform site.
- I recommend that you take measures to bug-proof the floor decking. One good solution is to apply Tyvek building membrane under the decking above the joists as a barrier.
- After construction, coat all surfaces with a high-quality tung-oil finish to protect the wood from moisture and stains.

The woodstove: The woodstove installed in my tent is manufactured by Cylinder Stoves. The stove package is an ingenious design meant to be very portable with the option for an oven! All pieces of the chimney, the legs, and the warming shelf, as well as the detachable stainless-steel hot water reservoir, nest neatly inside the firebox for transport or storage. Try CylinderStoves.com.

If you're a beginner carpenter, you'll need help with these plans. I decided it would take too many pages for me to provide a working "beginner" narrative in conjunction with the drawings on these two pages. But to the experienced eye, these plans will make sense. In fact, don't be afraid to get creative. Some of my wall tents are on a steep hill, requiring the front to be built on stilts. Some have bigger decks, and one recedes into a hillside. Use scrap lumber if you have access to some.

If you want to leave your wall tent up all winter, you can drape clear plastic from a roll up and over the top so the snow will slide off easily. Canvas has a tendency to grab snow. (Or you can buy a vinyl rain fly to begin with and construct a frame for it (p.60) and avoid the problem altogether.) When I spent the winter in a wall tent, I rolled both ends of clear plastic around logs the length of the tent from front to back. For this model, you'll need to cut slits to accommodate the guy lines and use four smaller logs instead of one long one. As the snow piles up on the outside, it gets warmer on the inside, like an igloo.

Front View

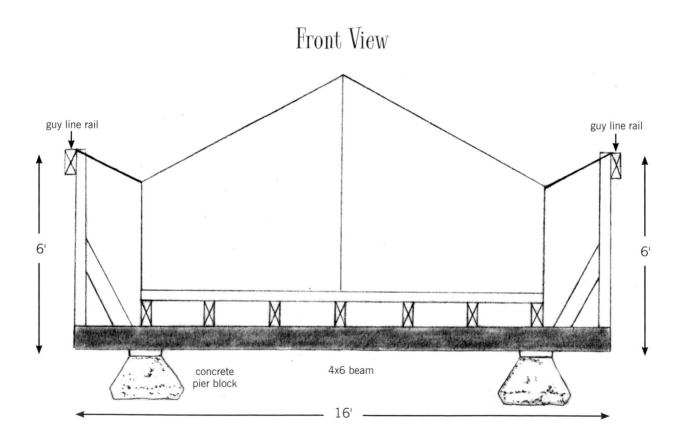

guy line rail

guy line rail

6'

6'

concrete pier block

4x6 beam

16'

Side View

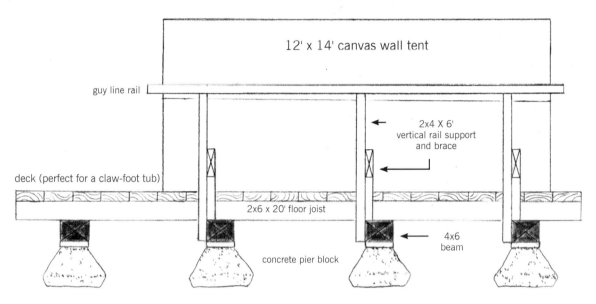

12' x 14' canvas wall tent

guy line rail

2x4 X 6' vertical rail support and brace

deck (perfect for a claw-foot tub)

2x6 x 20' floor joist

4x6 beam

concrete pier block

Top View

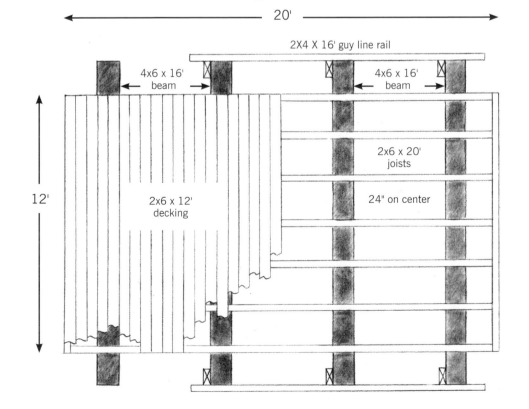

20'

2X4 X 16' guy line rail

4x6 x 16' beam

4x6 x 16' beam

12'

2x6 x 12' decking

2x6 x 20' joists

24" on center

wall tent grommet in peak, one on each end

½"-thick steel pin holding column to the ridge protrudes through grommet in top of wall tent

tent canvas

2x4 ridge inside tent canvas

vertical inner 2x4 support column

Rain Fly Frame Supply List

1	2x4 x 16'	ridge
18	2x4 x 10'	rafters
1	2x4	spacing block
9	12" lengths	plumber's tape
1	pound	truss-head screws or roofing nails
1	pound	16-penny galvanized nails

duct tape

24 fender washers

The tent's rain fly is made of reinforced vinyl sized 2' longer and 2' wider than the tent to provide some additional overhang. The stove chimney roof jack is located directly above the tent's chimney jack. Both chimney flashings have a weather flap for use when the chimney is removed in the off-season.

The 2x4 rafters and ridge lie flat and are supported by the inner tent ridge and the outside guy rail. For this 12' x 14' wall tent, the ridge piece is a 16'-long 2x4 and there are eighteen 10'-long 2x4 rafters.

First, the distance between the protruding ½" steel pins atop the tent was measured, and corresponding ¾" holes were bored through the 16'-long ridge. The ridge is held in place by the pins. The upper end of each rafter is cut 18° to match the slope of the tent peak in relation to where the lower ends of the rafters will lie—in this case, the outer guy line rail.

The rafter tops are joined together with a 12" length of metal plumber's tape using 1" truss-head screws or roofing nails to make a low-profile connection. A 2x4 block is placed between the 18° rafter ends. This block simulates the flat-lying ridge over which the plumber's tape (sometimes called "hanger tape") will span once the opposing rafter pairs are in place. Once all rafters are spaced about 24" apart, the length the fly will span, their tails are secured to the guy line rail with 16-penny galvanized nails. At the peak, the plumber's tape and fasteners are covered with duct tape to prevent the fly fabric from chafing where it contacts the metal hardware.

After all rafters are properly spaced and securely fastened, the fly is draped over the rafters, centered, then held down using more 1" screws and fender washers. The larger-diameter fender washers help relieve the strain of this intermittent fastening of fabric to a rigid surface.

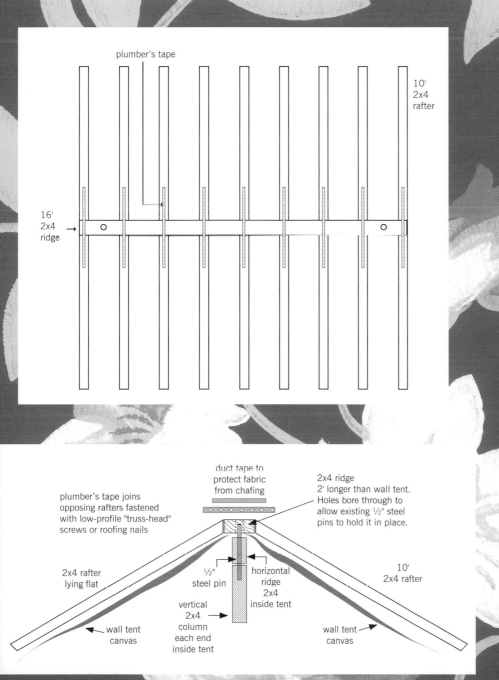

plumber's tape

10'
2x4
rafter

16'
2x4
ridge

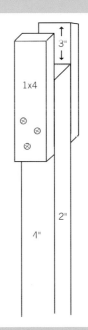

1x4

3"

2"

1"

For winter snow, we also made two removable support columns to erect inside the tent that cradle and support the ridge about a third of the way toward the center. The 2x4s that make these support columns are cut to the same length as the existing ridge columns at each end.

duct tape to protect fabric from chafing

plumber's tape joins opposing rafters fastened with low-profile "truss-head" screws or roofing nails

2x4 ridge 2' longer than wall tent. Holes bore through to allow existing ½" steel pins to hold it in place.

2x4 rafter lying flat

½" steel pin

horizontal ridge 2x4 inside tent

10' 2x4 rafter

vertical 2x4 column each end inside tent

wall tent canvas

wall tent canvas

Ready, Set, Pitch a Tent

Sure, you have a trailer, and she's a dandy. For better or for worse, you two are hitched. She welcomes your road-weary bones and shelters you from the whims of weather.

But every now and then, a rambling rose needs her space. Big space. Wide open, breeze blowin', birds chirpin' kind of space.

That's why you stow a tent in your trailer.
Yup, a tent.

No, you're not too old to sleep on the ground (that's what a plush little camping mattress is for—not even spring chickens want to rest on rubble. See p. 66).

And don't worry, your trusty trailer won't mind it if you stray for a night. Heck, she probably appreciates a little space too!

No more excuses.

Butters family, Yellowstone National Park, 1956

Get ready ...

A special evening will surprise you out there on the road (or even your backyard). The sunset will bow gracefully to the first twinkling stars, the wind will be warm, and crickets will start singing their hearts out. That's when you'll feel it:

I don't want to go inside tonight!

Up for a challenge?

Get out your heavy-duty sewing machine (mine is a Sailrite Ultrafeed LSZ-1, Sailrite.com). Instructions and supplies for my tent are online at www.MaryJanesFarm. org/Recipes-Patterns-Instructions/tent_ instructions.pdf.

Get set ... No worries. You're a big girl. You make the rules (or break 'em). Cast curfew to the wind. It's time to ...

Pitch a tent!

The sheer walls of a tent provide privacy and bug protection, but you still get to experience all the incredible sounds and scents of nature at night. And there's nothing like waking up to bright-and-early bird songs in stereo. You'll never want to rise to the clamor of a clock radio again.

Set Up Camp

A little care when choosing a campsite will result in a lot more comfort throughout the night.

- Look for level ground that isn't too rough and bumpy. Soft grass and sand are dreamy—rocks are not.
- Scrape away loose bits of gravel, sticks, and pinecones with your shoe or a small rake.
- Lay a ground cloth or tarp, folding it to fit neatly beneath your tent. Exposed tarp edges can collect rain or dew and channel it under your tent.
- Pop your tent into place and start nesting.

Remember that camping mattress I mentioned earlier? I knew you wouldn't forget.

A good mattress is crucial to a restful night's sleep while in a tent. Don't skimp. Cheap air mattresses lose their air and those cheap foam pads from the discount store will leave you so sore and exhausted that not even the sweetest bird songs will cheer you up in the morning.

Some glampers prefer air mattresses like the AerobedPakmat Airbed, available at Cabelas.com and Amazon.com. And it doesn't hurt that it's a peppy shade of bright green. Too cute! It inflates quickly with a hand pump that doubles as the bed's carrying case. Plus, unlike other vinyl air cushions, the Pakmat's plastic does not contain toxic phthalates.

I like Therm-a-Rest mattresses. I've had one for 30 years that also makes into a chair. But now that my bones are a little older, I invested in a Therm-a-Rest DreamTime Mattress. It's thicker, has a layer of memory foam, and self-inflates. Shockingly comfortable! Available at LLBean.com. Make sure to read online reviews to find the mattress that's best for you.

> " O Bed! Oh Bed! Oh delicious Bed!
> That heaven on earth for the weary head. "
>
> – Thomas Hood

Once your mattress is inflated, you can unfurl your sleeping bag or bring the blankets from your trailer to keep you cozy. The benefit of a sleeping bag is that you're fully surrounded with warmth, although a hot summer night may call for only a light quilt.

Porch & Garden Glamping

A shouldin' I should go, a shouldin' I should go, hi-ho the ...

Shouldering the shoulds in life can wear us down. That's where porch and garden glamping come in. They're your designated should-free zones—a go-to place all yours.

I have a glamping buddy who takes her laptop to her trailer (parked in her driveway) and locks the door. How about a canvas lean-to that has a "nap" cot? Although you're probably only a few feet from your door, you can pretend you're miles away. Rooftop glamping anyone?

What is it about a hammock?

I think I know. It has something to do with promise. The promise that you might, you probably will, slow down, sometime. In the back yard or the back 40 (as in my case), my hammock waits for me to come. Even if I don't keep my end of the promise to rendezvous, I need to know it's THERE, waiting for me. It gently tugs at my thoughts, often at the most hectic moments, and beckons daydreams of time spent swaying in escape. With my body comfortably cradled and feet resting from all the demands of the ground below, I savor the view: tree limbs dancing and clouds billowing across the blue sky at a pace I long to live by each day, every hour. Maybe that's why a hammock is such a special place to be. It reminds us, however briefly we may visit it, that these unhurried moments of reverie may always be found in its fold.

Here's a quick and easy, but romantic, hammock fashioned from "upcycled" curtains that takes only minutes to make.

1. Stitch bottoms of heavy, lined curtains together with heavy thread. Make two rows of stitching to ensure a durable seam.

2. Cut two lengths of heavy rope that has a load limit of 324 lbs (or more, if needed); double and knot the loose ends.

3. Wrap end of one length of rope around a tree and pull the knotted end through to secure.

4. Make a lark's-head knot as shown above, and leave loop open to insert one end of hammock fabric.

5. Make a simple overhand knot in one end of the hammock fabric.

6. Insert one end of the hammock fabric through the lark's head knot loop.

7. Pull lark's head knot taut to secure the end.

8. Optional: Tuck and hide the end of the rope inside the fabric knot. Repeat steps 3–8 for the other end.

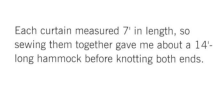

Each curtain measured 7' in length, so sewing them together gave me about a 14'-long hammock before knotting both ends.

Housekeeping

IDEAL FOR SILKS, HOSIERY AND LINGERIE
OR HANDKERCHIEFS

JUST THE RIGHT SIZE TO FIT A BUCKET,
PAIL OR LAVATORY

PACKS EASILY INTO SUIT CASE
OR TRAVELING BAG

COLUMBUS WASHBOARD CO., COLUMBUS, OHIO

"I am a
marvelous
housekeeper.

Every time I leave a man,
I keep his house."

— Zsa Zsa Gabor

IN THIS CHAPTER

Trailer Trash

Whoa, Nellie! Before you get the giggles or take offense at what may appear to be crude humor, let me assure you, the term "trailer trash" is serious business for the gal on the go. Mind you, the gal is not the trash to which I'm referring (come on, you know me better than that).

I'm talking genuine garbage, refuse, waste matter, and whatnot.

(We'll talk about the whatnots later.)

The thing is, even when you scale down to live on the loose, you still end up with leftovers. It's unavoidable. And I'll be the first to admit that even the most inspired upcycler can't repurpose *everything*.

This leads us to the dilemma of disposal. If it can't be reused (a plastic meat package, for instance), then it needs to be pitched properly. I'd love to tell you that the days of pitching beer cans out the windows of speeding cars are blessedly behind us. However, more than 51 billion pieces of litter land on U.S. roadways every year (that's 6,729 items per mile). Yuck, right? Littering is unladylike, to say the least. But trust me when I tell you that even sanitation can be accomplished in style.

So, how does a green-minded glamper ditch her disposables?

Recycling on the Road

Yes, you really can recycle while rambling. A simple online search, available at Earth911.com, will reveal garbage recycling centers galore along your route. I searched for a place to pitch plastic beverage bottles near little ol' Lyle, Washington, and I got a list of seven sites. Add recycling centers to your itinerary so you won't get stuck wondering where to go with your waste.

Dumping Do's

If you can't find a recycling center along your route, trash cans abound where passersby can legally "pitch in" without paying a dime. Gas stations, rest stops, campgrounds, and parks often offer trash cans to accommodate car clean-outs. My advice? Take advantage of every refuse repository you encounter to keep your trailer tidy.

Dumping Don'ts

If you stop to fill up on gas and find the station's trash cans overflowing, wait to deposit your waste at the next stop. Placing your trash beside the bin is technically considered littering—who knew? Also, resist the temptation to unload your trash in dumpsters owned by restaurants, hotels, apartment complexes, and other businesses that don't take kindly to public dumping and may even press charges.

BYOB
(Bring Your Own Bins)

Start your journey smelling like roses by toting a top-notch trash bin in your trailer. Of course, size matters—you don't want to take up your entire mobile mansion with a garbage pail. All you need is some sort of sturdy plastic container with a lid that seals tight (a must for transporting stuff that may present the "P.U." factor before you find a dump site). One handy-dandy option is a 5-gallon farm-style bucket from PleasantHillGrain.com with a Gamma Seal Lid that renders the bucket both air- and water-tight. Keeping it clean is your choice. Line your bucket with biodegradable trash bags (BioBagUSA.com) or spritz it with white vinegar and wipe clean as needed.

Vintage canister sets are ideal for compost.

Attention, die-hard composters (I know you're out there).

Stow an odor-free kitchen compost container, like the 1-gallon stainless-steel cutie from Norpro.com, to catch fruit and veggie scraps left over after meals.

Waste Not, Want Not

Taking your tiny home on the road means tightening up—there's no room for excess. Your new sense of simplification can be applied to trash, too. With a dash of forethought, you'll cut down on waste before it even begins to pile up.

Reduce packaging associated with carryout food by declining bags and boxes whenever possible.

Carry a reusable mug to avoid disposable cups.

Keep a cooler packed with fresh food from farm stands and grocery stores. You'll get more dinner for your dollar and a lot less packaging to pitch.

Le Toilet

When Nature Calls

The topic of the, ah, *toilet* may not be a glamorous one (although saying it in French does seem to give it a glint of glam).

- - - - - - - - - - - - - - - - - - - -

Seriously, though, every girl on the go needs to know where she will, in fact, go when nature calls. There's no denying it—nature will call. She always does.

Tote-able Toilet Seat and Lid

Shop: Amazon.com
Price: Roughly $15

- Turns an ordinary 4¼-, 5- or 6-gallon bucket into a portable toilet.

Toilet Waste Bags

Shop: Amazon.com, Cabelas.com
Price: Roughly $18

- Easy, no-mess waste disposal.
- Inner and outer bag that is sealable and leak-proof.
- Pre-charged with Bio-Gel that solidifies liquid waste and masks unpleasant odors.

Few trailers, if any, are decked out with built-in bathrooms. After all, we're not talking about tour buses or mobile mansions here. The compact cuties I love simply don't have room for full-fledged facilities. Not to worry, though.

For the most part, the gypsy glamper will be within reach of a rest stop, gas station, or campground, should she hear the call. The proverbial "pit-stop" is generally a quick and painless affair. But, say you find yourself on a desolate stretch of road, or you land upon a loo that's less than, shall we say, comfortable. Or maybe, you wake up in the middle of the night to a cold rain and you simply can't muster the gumption to get out and trek to the nearest public restroom. In these instances, a wise wanderer will rest assured, knowing that she is prepared with her own private potty.

"No way."

That was my first reaction years ago.

"Get OUT!" came in a close second.

Curious?

Well, then, you asked.

I'm alluding to the …
GoGirl or the Freshette. What's a GoGirl, you ask? As the name spiritedly (if somewhat surreptitiously) implies, the GoGirl is … let me check their website again to see how they frame it …

"A female urination device (FUD)."

For real.

Who knows? It may just become your best friend, Miss Fuddy-Duddy.

Here's how the GoGirl site defines the device:

"Simply put, GoGirl is the way to stand up to crowded, disgusting, distant, or non-existent bathrooms. It's a female urination device that allows you to urinate while standing up. It's neat. It's discreet. It's hygienic."

So tasteful it almost qualifies as table talk. Well … almost.

But, seriously, I have encountered situations in which the GoGirl has saved me untold embarrassment. I remember the time …

Right, we won't even GO there. (Well, maybe for just a minute.)

How about when a guy on the road has to pee at night and there's no rest stop in sight? Easy. Pull over and stand there, discreetly checking the air in the front passenger tire. If a pair of headlights hit, he turns ever so slightly, averting his …

No problem. Done.

For a girl, those headlights illuminate a full moon. Should your caught-off-guard embarrassment stop you mid-stream, well, we all know the consequences of a mid-stream stop. And what girl hasn't risked life and limb by hiking into the bushes in a pair of high heels? Lions, tigers, and bears, oh my.

Or if I'm in a place where I'm uncomfortable leaving my car, I pull out my Freshette FUD with its 48-inch extension tube (when it comes to locker room talk, I rank), crack the door open, and aim it outside and onto the ground. Done. If I'm in a situation where it's not cool to "leave my mark," my Freshette comes with a pack of sturdy plastic EMPTY (soon to be full) urine bags that I dispose of once home.

And, ewwwh, how about public restrooms? For the longest time, I did the full-muscle crouch to avoid contact with the seat UNTIL that time in a big city when my pee was hitting the waist of my pants the entire time and filling up my dressy, black, tuxedo skinny jeans pant leg. Never again.

For first-time glampers, it's THE handy dandy tool for ladies who aren't crazy about crouching in the woods. Glamour camping all the way. Go, little pink! (FUDs are generally pink.)

Made of medical-grade silicone, the GoGirl tucks flexibly into a purse, pocket, or glove compartment. And, yes, it's reusable. As the manufacturer clarifies, "Urine is sterile, but the product can come into contact with contaminants during use, so take precautions when cleaning." Wash well with hot, soapy water, or clean with a handy wipe, dry thoroughly, and you're good to …

… GoGirl!

Buy it at Amazon, Cambria Bicycle Outfitter, or Bass Pro Shops for about $10. Then visit the GoGirl website (Go-Girl.com) to learn how to use it. (No demos. I'm not going there. It's a private matter.)

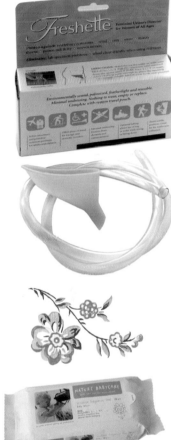

Rapid Bath

Glamping got a whole lot easier once wipettes were invented. Fragrance-free wipes from Nature Babycare are a great allergen-free way to wash your face, then a quick wipe "down under" and into the campfire. Naty.com

Go Anywhere Portable Toilet

Shop: Cleanwaste PETT Portable Toilet: REI.com,
Backcountry.com, Campmor.com, Amazon.com
Price: $80 to $280 (basic pot or full kit)

Specs:

- Tripod frame unfolds from a briefcase-sized block into the same height and bowl dimensions as a standard toilet
- Outhouse privacy shelter (tent) comes with the full kit
- Removable mesh holder supports biodegradable waste-collection WAG BAG bag
- Eco-friendly Pooh Powder turns liquid waste into an odorless solid
- WAG BAG waste bags are landfill approved and can be disposed of in trash with regular garbage
- Permitted by the U.S. Bureau of Land Management for use on rivers and in Wilderness Areas where toilets are required
- Recommended by the Leave No Trace program
- Extra WAG BAGS and Pooh Powder sold separately

hoity-toity tent

Think you can't "go" without a toilet for any length of time?

Consider this. When I left home at age 18, I lived without an indoor flush toilet for 23 consecutive years, 30 total. I feel a little bit like the woman I heard about who couldn't reach her clothesline so she moved a stool around her entire life. I should have done it sooner, but new septic regulations came with a price tag that was close to $10,000. That's a lot of money when merely moving a stool around will get the job done. (Word play is such fun.)

Besides, early on, I found a pink wicker potty in an antique store that was clearly more adorable than a porcelain throne.

But I must confess, sometimes I said under my breath (while trudging through torrential rains or blinding snowstorms carrying my chamber pot), "SOMEDAY, I will have it easy like everyone else."

Everyone else. Isn't that always what keeps us from true gratitude? Others have it better—better health, more money, less worry, more vacation days … Well, I'd like to point out something you've probably missed when you're feeling less than queenly—your throne! The next time I'm forgetting gratefulness for all the little things that make my life easier, my reminder is now only a few steps away. The moral to this story? Spending a few days without a flush toilet will give you good material for your gratitude journal.

Laundry & Bathing

When I say the word "camping," what images come to mind?

Fresh air? **Yes!**

Campfire? **Love it.**

Dirt? **Well, sure.**

Grubby hair, grungy clothes, greasy napkins? **Okay, now we need to talk …**

If camping makes you cringe, conjuring notions of hampered hygiene, I'm here to tell you, sister, that "glamping" is a whole new game.

Around my campfire, it's not unusual to find glossy curls and freshly laundered flannel. Don't be surprised, either, if I break out a dainty lace doily on which to rest my cup and saucer. Forget prissy—this is about playfulness and pleasure. A girl doesn't have to compromise her style to get out and go wild.

Laundering

RV-friendly campsites often offer coin-operated laundry facilities, but I'd like to fill you in on a nifty technique for scrubbing your duds that requires only a dash of effort. Save your quarters and conserve electricity—it's time to twist and shout and let your backbone slip.

You'll Need:
- Dry bag (Dry bags are used by river runners to keep their gear dry; try a 30L SealLine See Bag. Price: Roughly $30 from Amazon.com)
- Biodegradable liquid laundry soap
- Clothesline and pins

1. Fill your dry bag with laundry until it's about half full (one full outfit or several under-items will fit nicely).
2. Pour about 1 gallon of cool water into the bag.
3. Add 2 T biodegradable liquid laundry soap.
4. Seal up your bag per its instructions.
5. Shake, shimmy, swish, and twist your bag (shout and sing as desired) for about 5 minutes.
6. Open the bag and dispose of the soapy water at least 100 feet from any natural water source (lake or stream).
7. Wring out the clothes, pour in another gallon of water, and repeat steps 1 through 6 until laundry is soap-free.
8. Line-dry as you would at home.

Showering

When researching campgrounds where you plan to stop along your journey, you can pin down parks that offer shower facilities for free or, occasionally, a small fee. While a campground shower is not as luxurious as your own at home (a sturdy pair of waterproof sandals is a must), you'll revel in the indulgence of hot water while on the road.

Of course, the daring do-it-herself glamper can tote her own little camp shower along in her trailer that will allow her the luxury of cleaning up at her convenience, provided there is water available from a spigot or stream. Skip the myriad so-so shower models on the market, and head straight for top-of-the-line:

Zodi Outback Gear Camping Shower
Shop: Zodi.com, Amazon.com, Cabelas.com, BassPro.com
Price: $30 to $340 (depending upon the model and accessories)
Specs (for the Hot Tap Model, which sells for about $170):
- propane burner
- 6-volt pump (requires 4 "D" batteries)
- 4-gallon water tank (enough for up to a 10-minute shower)
- lightweight and compact designs
- privacy shelters (tents) available (see tent p. 80)

> How about a solar shower? Try Seattle Sports Camp Shower at Amazon.com. Roughly $15.

It's been years since I've taken a shower. "What, you say??"

Don't get me wrong, I'm not opposed to cleanliness. It's just that if I'm going to spend the time it takes to scrub my skin and launder my hair, I'm going to turn it into an affair that is completely opposite of the rest of my day. A shower has rushing water and the feel of hurry. I need something calming, restoring—a break that gives me pause. Float time. Close my eyes time.

Step back with me to the year 1973 ...

I've been in my hiking boots portaging a 40-pound backpack for most of a day. I'm hiking alone above timberline in the Uinta Mountain Range of Utah, where I'm working as a Wilderness Ranger. Working outside has trained me to be okay with the fact that heat has a mind of its own. In other words, I lost the argument early on that hot summer day. The natural world is even harsher above where trees can grow—they decline for good reason. I come to a rise where centuries of unrelenting winds have carved two-foot-deep depressions into the rock. Unbelievably, from a recent cloudburst, the "bathtubs" are full of sun-warmed, clean, rain water.

You might have heard my sigh when I dropped my backpack and drawers, pulled off my swealy socks and lowered my tired body into the kind of bliss I've never forgotten—a craving that would stay with me all these years.

Trying to recapture that moment, that ahhhh, I bought a hot tub.

But keeping the water clean was work; keeping it heated was wasteful. More important, it wasn't a bath. I couldn't give myself a scrub-down. Still seeking a solution, it came to me one day,

"A tub is just an oversized cast-iron cooking pot. Why couldn't I put one outside and light a fire under it?"

Once I started collecting old cast-iron claw-foot bathtubs and figured out how to heat them easily,

I've recaptured that 1973 bath moment over and over again. My daughter embroidered her favorite quote in red on a large piece of canvas that I have hanging by one of my tubs: "Remember, you were once wild. You bathed in the open."

My bed and breakfast guests get in on it, too, because each of my five wall-tent units are equipped with a bathtub out the back flap. And with a garden hose that is frost-free for filling any of my seven tubs (placed just so, here and there around my farm) with fresh water in the winter, I can also find bath bliss during a snowstorm; after a hard day at work; when I need to make an important decision; when I need to sort, to sift, and remember ... I was once wild.

Bath accoutrements are essential. If you're bathing indoors, try to take the plunge with your bathroom window open. The sounds of the outside seem to go hand in hand with bathing.

I was staying in a hotel in New York City during my first book tour in 2005 when I did just that. I threw open a window and heard a songbird, perched on a fire escape, singing its little heart out—bath bliss again. At that moment in my life, so far away from home, the hot, steamy water and the immersion were like a baptism of sorts. Bliss can be found anywhere, I realized. Just open the window and let it in. In a pinch, buy a songbird CD. Audubon sells them. Or pick up flute music infused with the sound of a bubbling brook. Crickets. Thunderstorms and soft rain. All of nature has been recorded.

Lighting needs to be soft or none at all. Candles, candles, and more candles. The flickering flame of a candle is hypnotic. It's that wild thing again. Not so very long ago, our forebears spent their evenings staring into campfires. For decadence, there's wine, chocolate, or bubbles—or all three when the going gets rough. And don't forget essential oils. Put a few drops of lavender directly into the water, or the essence of pine or sage. Float a fresh flower.

It's time ...
Your time.

Riggin' Up a Glamping Bathtub

Time: approximately 3 hours
Skill Level: beginner–intermediate

Think of your cast-iron bathtub as a giant cooking pot. You can simply build a wood fire under the tub to heat the water, but I devised a permanent "fire" by using a propane camp stove.

YOU'LL NEED:
• 6 12" x 12" concrete pavers (optional)
• cast-iron tub
• 2-burner propane camp stove (I use the heavy-duty cast-iron two-burner stove from HurricaneProducts.net)
• 6' (or more) flexible gas line
• 5-gallon or larger propane bottle with regulator
• Adjustable wrench (opens to at least 1")

1. Lay concrete pavers on a level, undisturbed 2' x 3' piece of ground or deck.
2. Position your tub on top of the pavers and your camp stove underneath the tub.
3. Attach the gas line to the propane stove on one end and to the propane bottle on the other end. (If you decide to hide the propane tank, you can build a small wooden box around it. Make sure the box you build has a couple of air vents in the sides.)
4. If the area where you're situating your bathtub is prone to wind, you can do one of two things: build an unmortared brick wall around the tub on three sides with numerous gaps for air flow, or build a skirt around the tub on three sides out of metal flashing. Either way, be sure to leave gaps large enough to allow access to valves for lighting, air, and regulation.

Word of Caution: Propane isn't for sissies. You need to know what you're doing. Now that propane is such a big part of recreational activities, make sure you know the ins and outs. If there's any doubt, hire a professional—someone in your area who works on propane appliances.

If you're really on top of things, you've traded in your spray bottle full of soapy water (for making sure your propane gas connections are snug and up to snuff) for a professional portable gas-leak detector. Good idea also for that care-free backyard propane gas barbeque you love so much.

I fill the bathtub with fresh water from a garden hose, light the burners underneath the tub, then check the water temperature in about two hours (depending on the outside temperature). If you want to speed this process up, you can put a piece of plywood on top, cut to size. Once I'm ready for my bath, I turn off both burners and hop in (I touch the bottom of the tub first to make sure it's not too hot, and don't ever step directly on top of the burner areas). If the water is too hot, I use my hose to add a little cold water. And since I use only biodegradable soaps, I simply pull the plug and let the water run out onto the ground when my bath is finished.

Ahhhhhh ...

A pine bath can be intoxicating. Using a 1' square of muslin, put the tips of pine branches in the center, tie to secure, and put it in your bath water while it heats. Confession: I float an entire branch in mine—remove it just before you step in, adding drops of pine essential oil and lighting a pine-scented candle.

Winterizing Your Trailer

Like all good things, glamping season must come to an end.

And just like you, your pretty little trailer needs some time to rest and rejuvenate after all that trekking from glampout to glampout.

We all know we're not supposed to put ourselves to bed without taking off our makeup first, and the same is true for your pretty little trailer. You should never put your trailer to bed without a little prep for the long, cold months ahead.

Clean 'er Up
A bedtime bath is a good idea. Not only to have her sitting pretty all winter, but also to avoid any damage that dirt, grease, and grime might do over time. It's most important, however, to clean out the inside. An obvious one is to remove all food, including canned items, but you might also want to leave the fridge, cupboard doors, drawers, closets, etc. open. It'll give them a chance to air out, and a good ol' box of baking soda will help to mitigate any musty smells when you're once again ready to roll.

Save the Charge
I think it's best to remove your beauty's battery before you store her for the winter. The idea is to make sure things stay clean and in working order 'til your next glamping adventure, and you don't want to deal with the mess of corroded battery connections when you're excited to get back on the road.

Empty It Out
The most important winterizing task you'll have is emptying out the water tanks and plumbing. A busted-up pipe can be a bummer come summer. You'll want your water tanks and lines to be completely empty for winter storage—and, yes, this means taking on the less-than-glamorous job of making sure your black water (i.e., sewage) tank is emptied.

Blow It Out

Once the tanks are empty, you can use compressed air to blow air through the water system to rid it of any remaining water. Purchase a blow-out plug (CampingWorld.com), screw it into your water inlet, and attach an air compressor to the valve on the plug, being careful not to use pressure higher than 45 PSI. Open faucets, showerhead, etc., one by one, until only air comes out.

Or Anti-Freeze It

Another (faster) option to ensuring your water lines will hibernate safely through the winter is to add some non-toxic antifreeze to the tank and let it run through the system. Run the faucets and flush the toilet until the water is the same color (usually red) as the antifreeze.

No Sweat!

OK, girls, you know how we all love that dewy look that makes us glow like young girls freshly in love? Well, your sweet little trailer doesn't need that. When it comes to vintage trailers, condensation is not your friend. Moisture means mold. The worst thing you can do is cover your trailer with a tarp or plastic sheet. Metal needs air circulation or heat to keep it happy and dry. This can be especially important in wetter climates. The dryer the climate, the less you need to worry; but in a moist climate, you should be particularly careful. If you can, pamper your glamper by storing it in a heated garage or storage space, or leave a tiny space heater inside on low (be sure to check on it periodically).

FRESH WATER

Keep Out Critters

As soon as you move out, the mice will try to move in. Messy, smelly, and destructive—rodents are not good glampers. You will want to do what you can to keep them out of your trailer when it's not in use. Plug up any possible entry points with steel wool. Make sure you check out all vents and gaps, even those underneath the trailer, and keep in mind that mice can squeeze through the tiniest of holes. As for the inside, some folks swear by smelly dryer sheets (think Bounce), but others say that after a while, the mice just use them for a nest. You can also try cotton balls with drops of peppermint oil, or an all-natural product such as Fresh Cab Rodent Repellent (Earth-Kind.com).

Décor Ideas

Decorate a room of my own? Oh my, yes.

This alone may be the reason women are so attracted to trailers—that and the fact that our inner gypsy needs an outlet. Not to mention our love of vintage. Toss in our love of home, retro anything, color, and nostalgia, and you have … TRAILER. I call them glampers, folks in the UK call them caravans, but whatever you call them, I promise, a glamper is the perfect escape.

But how to style it? You've hunted down your special "someone." Now it's time to gussy her up.

Some owners adhere to a strict remake in the era their glamper was born, but I like to go junktiquing, tiny detail by tiny detail. Word of caution: the treasure hunt to fill a glamper ends all too soon. (After all, they're small.) Savor every detail. Take your time.

When I style anything, I like to start with just one object, or a group of objects, that make my heart sing. From there, a'collectin' I will go. Colors, era, all of it falls into place from there. Having your glamper ethos defined from the get-go will land you right where you want to end up. I designed an entire guest cabin around one teacup I found in an antique store. I even painted the design from the teacup onto the floor.

1964 Safari with rear door (rare), perfect for the gypsy wagon owned by Sharon Lambert and painted by James Jackson, an art teacher in Mississippi, who used latex exterior house paint and photos of gypsy wagons in the UK for inspiration.

Imagine my surprise when I found this organic cotton sheet set by Amy Butler in my local Bed, Bath, and Beyond store. Be still, my heart.

Dark pink and light green with flamingo décor? Total retro.

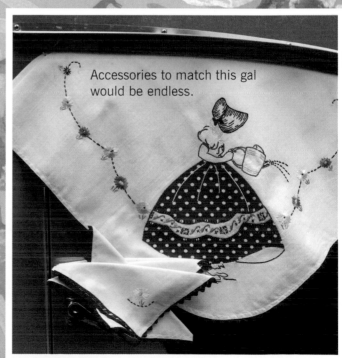

Wouldn't a trailer in these colors be as sweet as can be?

Mustard yellow and black? I can see it now.

Accessories to match this gal would be endless.

"The ache for home lives in all of us,
the safe place where we can go as
we are and not be questioned."

— Maya Angelou

Space can be tight in a trailer, so a good glamper adores things that can do double—or triple—duty. How about a magazine rack and rolling stool all in one?! For the base, you'll need a square or rectangular rolling plant caddie, available at any garden supply center. Onto that, use two strong leather belts to secure a stack of magazines and a pillow. All-in-one seating, recycling, and storage. And, if your trip ever gets extended, you'll have plenty of reading material.

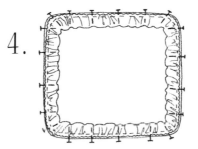

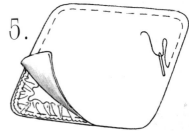

Dish-Drainer Quilt

I tried several different thicknesses of polyester batting when I first invented dish-drainer quilts. You'd think most anything would do, but I discovered that only low-loft batting works. And I prefer polyester over cotton because I like my dish-drainer quilts to dry quickly. (Notice I have quite a few!) If your quilt is too thick (and this can mean even an additional $\frac{1}{8}$" loft), things like drinking glasses want to tip over. My recommendation is June Tailor, Inc. quilter's fusible 100% polyester batting in low loft 36" x 45" craft size. I picked mine up at my local Jo-Ann Fabrics store. I also pre-washed all the fabrics I used for my dish-drainer quilts.

1. Cut two pieces of fabric 17" x 19" and round the corners. Cut one piece of batting the same size as the fabric. With your iron, fuse the batting to the wrong side of the top fabric.
2. For the ruffle, cut three $3\frac{1}{2}$"-wide strips of 40–45" fabric (cut crosswise, from selvage to fold).
3. Cut the ends of the ruffle strips at a slight angle before stitching together to prevent bulky seams. Stitch the three ruffle strips together to form one long strip, then stitch ends together to form a circle. Fold the long strip lengthwise, wrong sides together. Baste $\frac{1}{2}$" in from raw edge.
4. Gather the ruffle and pin it into place on the right side of the bottom piece, raw edges together (fold facing middle). Stitch ruffle to bottom piece, using a $\frac{1}{2}$" seam. (Make sure there's enough ruffle on the corners to lie smoothly when the ruffle is turned out.)
5. Place the top fabric on the bottom fabric, right sides together. Stitch, using a $\frac{1}{2}$" seam, leaving an opening for turning. Clip the corners.
6. Turn the mat right side out and hand-stitch the opening closed. Top stitch $\frac{1}{2}$" from the edge to finish.

Apron up your propane tank.

Other fun ideas ...

When you decorate your glamping space, don't neglect a matching skirt for your toilet.

Word to the wise: The simplest toilets are best (p. 76). Don't get hoodwinked into expensive models that compost or incinerate. Talk to people who've bought them. Read reviews. Word on the street is, they tend to be everyone's most expensive mistake.

Reboot

There are plenty of jokes about women buying a new pair of shoes or a purse to make themselves feel better. It's the purse-ability of bold colors, softer leather, glitter, an ostrich feather here, a lacy veil there, something big, or something dainty that pulls us in. Purses, shoes, and hats are adornments that cheer us up mainly because they cheer up those around us. The bigger the hat I wear to town, the more I make people smile. Tell me you don't smile when you see a group of women out and about wearing matching outfits adorned in feathers and sequins.

Bootleg Lamp

YOU'LL NEED:
boot (or a pair for matching end tables)
lamp-making kit
drill and drill bit (bit should be slightly
    larger than lamp-making kit's power cord)
steel nipples (enough to reach from
    bottom to top of boot, plus 1")
couplings
4" cross bar
locknut
level
sand (enough to fill boot)
FixAll patching compound
coordinating acrylic paint
paint brush
lampshade

1. Drill hole ½" from base of boot heel.
2. Using couplings, attach steel nipples together to form lamp rod. Attach one end of rod to 4" crossbar; secure with locknut.
3. Insert power cord through hole in boot heel, 4" crossbar, and lamp rod.
4. Assemble lamp following lamp-making kit directions.

5. Place lamp rod in boot; pull cord tight. Use level to determine proper rod placement. Slowly fill boot with sand to 3" from boot top.
6. Mix FixAll as directed on package; fill remaining 3" of boot. Smooth surface and let dry.
7. If desired, paint FixAll surface.
8. Add lampshade.

Ample Up Your Boots

What gal hasn't bought a pair of second-hand cowgirl boots that are too tight on her calves?

Here's a solution. Slice a slit in the back with a razor knife. Punch holes in the leather or add metal grommets if you're making your rubber mud boots bigger. Lace 'em up and tie 'em in a bow.

Crafty Glamper

Time to tie one on? You bet. A necktie, that is.
Give those shredded old lawnchairs a snazzy
spruce-up with colorful neckties. Just stretch
'em, weave 'em, stitch a few of 'em, and tie the
rest. Try the same thing with old leather belts.
So cute!

Birdhouse

Twig Basket

A twiggy bank is one way you can save up for a glamper.

Make sure there isn't easy access to your someday glamper money.

Reel Women "Hooked" on Fashion

Common fishing lures, available in most any sporting-goods store, are the perfect statement for reel women "hooked" on fashion. At once "alluring," they come with names hilariously perfect for the gal who's got the urge! Hobby stores sell everything you need to turn fishing lures into earrings, including beads to glue onto the ends of the barbed hooks.

Cyclone ... he'll never know what hit him

Pro-Glo Wedding Ring ... land a lunker

Sparkle Tail ... 'nuf said?

Hook & Smile Blade ... wait 'til we're married

Feel the Fight ... hooked on drama

Flutter ... heart-stopping

Stop & Go ... catch and release

Swinger ... multiple strikes

Have fun trolling! With a pair of alluring earrings, you'll have no problem reeling 'em in. For that next big catch, toss a line, then sink your hook into anything that nibbles.

Vintage fishing reels were made for storing earrings, right?

Glampsite Organizer
(hang a sweater or shoe organizer in a tree)

Glamping Potholders
Etsy.com/shop/BSoriginals

potholder photos courtesy of Shery Jespersen

Create Your Own Low-Impact Lighting

If you haven't made your own oil lamp, you're in for an enlightening experience. An oil lamp burns brightly and lasts for hours, lending a charming glow to your glampsite.

Olive-Oil Chandelier

Here's a simple project that uses half-pint, wide-mouth canning jars and household olive oil. Using the wire skeleton of an old lampshade and black annealed mechanic's wire (see p. 119), you can create a chandelier by wrapping wire around the threads of each jar and then attaching them to the ribs of the lampshade. Olive oil is smoke-free and odor-free. You can add a few drops of your favorite essential oil to scent your chandelier.

You'll need:
half-pint, wide-mouth canning jars
black annealed mechanic's wire
½–1" braided flat wick (try your local
   craft store or Lehmans.com)
olive oil

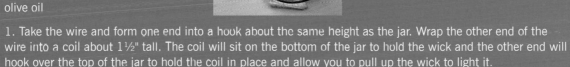

1. Take the wire and form one end into a hook about the same height as the jar. Wrap the other end of the wire into a coil about 1½" tall. The coil will sit on the bottom of the jar to hold the wick and the other end will hook over the top of the jar to hold the coil in place and allow you to pull up the wick to light it.
2. Put your wick into the coil with about ¼" sticking up above the coil and pinch the top of the coil to hold it (the other end of the wick will soak in the oil).
3. Add oil to the jar to just under the pinched coil.

Jar Lamp

You can buy a 100-hour survival candle (not really a candle, but a bottle lamp, see p. 121), or you can make one. Take a small canning jar and punch a hole from the inside of the lid in the center of the top using a 16-penny nail (short and squat jars are best because they're less likely to tip over). Purchase an ⅛" cotton wick and push no more than an ⅛" up through the hole, leaving several inches in the bottom of the jar. Fill the jar with paraffin lamp oil. Note: Use only small bottles; the wick can't draw the oil if the jar is too tall.

DIY Camp Stool, Table & Cot

Make a Camp Stool

Supply List

four	1x1 x 20"	legs
two	1x1 x 14"	horizontal seat braces
one	1x1 x 11½"	lower horizontal leg brace
one	1x1 x 9½"	lower horizontal leg brace
eight	⅜" x 1½"	dowels
two	2½" x ¼"	machine screws

four	¼"	washers
two	¼"	nylon locking nuts
canvas	9½" x apx. 22"	after hem is sewn along the 22" lengths

two dozen carpet tacks or upholstery tacks

carpenter's wood glue

Tools

small hammer

drill

¼" drill bit

⅜" drill bit

screwdriver

adjustable wrench or pliers

Each leg has four holes drilled into it. A $\frac{1}{4}$"-diameter hole is bored all the way through, 9" from the top, to accommodate a machine screw. Then a $\frac{3}{8}$"-diameter hole is bored 1" deep into the center of the end grain on the top of each leg. (This hole will accommodate a length of $\frac{3}{8}$" dowel to secure the horizontal seat brace.) Another $\frac{3}{8}$"-diameter hole is then bored halfway into each lower leg, $3\frac{1}{2}$" from the bottom of the leg, in line with the $\frac{1}{4}$" pivot hole.

Each lower horizontal leg brace is bored with a $\frac{3}{8}$"-diameter hole 1" deep into the center of the end grain. (Dowels will be glued into these to fasten them to each lower leg.)

The two horizontal seat braces each have two $\frac{3}{8}$"-diameter holes bored $\frac{1}{2}$" deep for dowels, both on the same side. (On one brace, the holes will be $1\frac{3}{4}$" from each end and $10\frac{1}{2}$" apart; on the other, the holes will be $\frac{3}{4}$" from each end and $12\frac{1}{2}$" apart. The difference in spacing is because the folding camp stool is made of two scissoring pairs of legs, one narrower than the other.)

Following the photos at right, tack the canvas to one seat brace, then roll the brace one revolution onto the canvas for strength (the holes that will hold the leg dowels need to end up on the bottom). Do the same with the second brace. When finished, the seat braces should be about 1' apart when the canvas is pulled taut to form a sturdy chair.

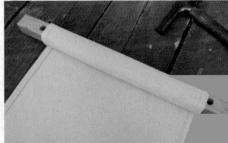

Assemble the legs using the screws, washers, and nuts. Attach the lower leg braces using dowels and glue. Attach the seat using dowels and glue.

Make a Camp Table   Portable and Collapsible

Supply List

one	1x12 x 6'	makes two 32"-long table-top halves.
two	2x2 x 8'	makes four 30" legs and one 19" horizontal brace
one	1x2 x 8'	makes two 18½" table-top supports
one	1x4 x 8'	makes two horizontal leg braces
two	¼" x 2" bolts	connect outer legs to table-top supports
two	¼" x 2½" bolts	connect outer legs to inner legs at the mid-length hinge point
14	¼" washers	under each bolt head and nut and between each hinge point
six	¼" locking nuts	locking-type nuts prevent loosening under repeated hinge action
20	1½" screws	to fasten table-tops to supports and leg braces

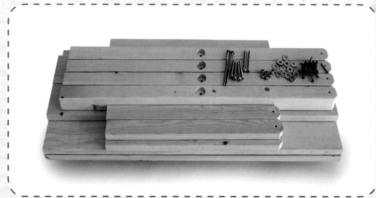

Note:
Table can be twice as long if you add a third set of legs.

(To see this table in action, see p. 211.)

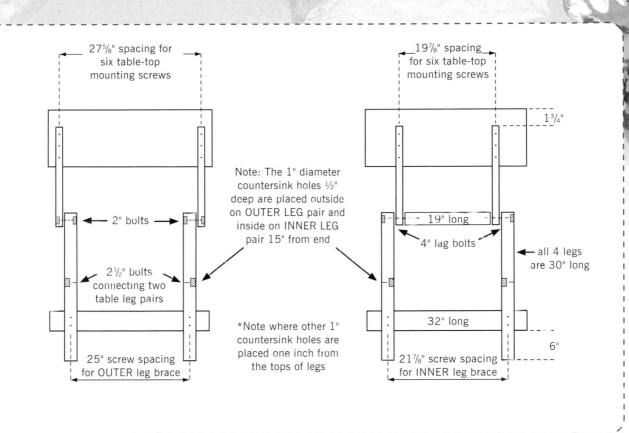

27⅝" spacing for six table-top mounting screws

2" bolts

2½" bolts connecting two table leg pairs

25" screw spacing for OUTER leg brace

Note: The 1" diameter countersink holes ½" deep are placed outside on OUTER LEG pair and inside on INNER LEG pair 15" from end

*Note where other 1" countersink holes are placed one inch from the tops of legs

19⅞" spacing for six table-top mounting screws

1¾"

19" long

4" lag bolts

all 4 legs are 30" long

32" long

6"

21⅞" screw spacing for INNER leg brace

Make a Camp Cot

collapsible with girly headboard & footboard

Supply List

four 2x2 x 8'

two 1x4 x 8'

one 1x12 x 8'

one 48" length each of $^{3}/_{16}$", $^{3}/_{8}$", and $^{3}/_{4}$" dowel stock

one bag of $^{1}/_{4}$" x 1$^{1}/_{4}$" fluted dowel pins

sandpaper, medium and fine

wood glue

hardwood accents for headboard and footboard

preshrunk heavyweight canvas, 37" x 72"

upholstery tacks

Cutting

Cut two 6'6" lengths of 2x2 for rails

Cut four 2'5$^{1}/_{2}$" lengths of 2x2 for legs

Cut one 4'2" length of 1x4 for sway support

Cut one 3'10$^{1}/_{2}$" length of 1x4 for sway support

Cut two 30" lengths of 1x12 for headboard and footboard

Cut four 7$^{1}/_{4}$" lengths of $^{3}/_{4}$" dowel for headboard and footboard attachments

Cut two 4" lengths of $^{3}/_{4}$" dowel for leg pivots

Cut four 2" lengths of $^{3}/_{8}$" dowel for headboard and footboard attachments

Cut four 1" lengths of $^{3}/_{16}$" dowel for headboard and footboard attachments

Tools

small level

tape measure

square

$^{1}/_{2}$" wood chisel

drill

$^{3}/_{16}$", $^{1}/_{4}$", $^{3}/_{8}$", and $^{3}/_{4}$" drill bits

hammer

fine-tooth hand saw or band saw

table saw

jigsaw

finished cot, all glammed up

(to collapse, remove headboard and footboard and fold)

1 On the rails, cut a ¾" mortise 14" from each end.

2 Drill a ¾" hole through each leg 14" from the floor end. The ¾" x 4" dowels will join the legs and provide a pivot point for folding the cot. Cut a ¾" tenon on the top end of each leg; this will join the legs to the rails. Cut a ¾" x 1½" half lap joint on the top inside of each leg, starting 7" from the floor end. These joints will receive the lengths of 1x4 for the leg sway supports.

3 The leg sway supports need a cut on each end for the half lap joint, leaving a 1½" tenon centered in the middle. The longer sway support goes between the outside legs, and the shorter one spans the inside legs. Once the half lap joints are in place, drill two ¼" holes through the sway support tenon into the leg to accept the ¼" x 1¼" fluted dowel pins.

4 Take the two 30" lengths of 1x12 for the headboard and footboard and decide what pattern you would like to cut. I made a simple pattern on a piece of butcher paper, cut it out, and traced the outline onto each board. Cut along your traced outline using the jigsaw. Use medium sandpaper to smooth out the saw marks. Drill ⅜" holes in the bottom corners of the boards 2½" in and 3" up. These will accept the ⅜" x 2" dowels you cut earlier.

5 The ⅜" dowels need a ³⁄₁₆" hole drilled ⅜" from one end. These holes will accept the ³⁄₁₆" x 1" dowels. Take the 7¼" lengths of ¾" dowels and cut a ⅜" hole 2" from one end. You can then take the ⅜" dowel with the ³⁄₁₆" keeper and push it through the ¾" dowel with the hole in it and into the hole in the corners of the headboard and footboard. This dowel setup will attach the headboard and footboard to the rails. The section of the ⅜" dowel that goes into the headboard and footboard will be glued. The ¾" dowel needs to be free to pivot.

6 Drill ¾" holes in the rails 2" from each end straight up and down to attach the headboard and footboard. I set the cot up and tied a cord in the middle of a rail, opened up the cot until the rails were 25" apart, and tied off the end of the cord to the other rail to hold everything in place while I marked the placement of the holes on the rails. To get the mark straight up and down, I used a small level held on the end of the rails and marked the line I wanted the bit to follow. Then I notched a spot where the hole would start to make the surface level. I made the notch big enough to receive the headboard and footboard so they sit level when they are attached.

7 Sand all of the pieces with fine sandpaper to remove any sharp corners and splinters. Glue all of the joints except the ¾" dowels that attach the headboard and footboard to the rails. I also left the ¾" dowels that act as pivots for the legs unglued.

8 Attach accents. Paint cot. Attach canvas to the underside of the rails using upholstery tacks.

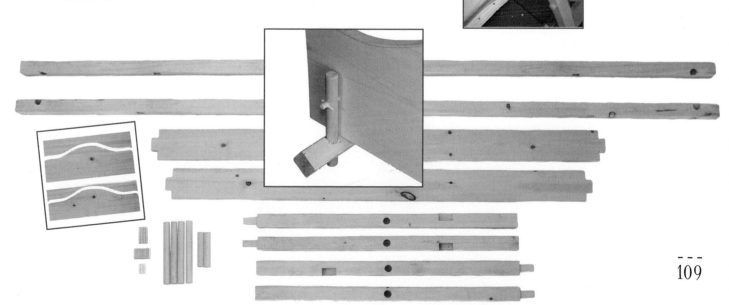

Gear

"When preparing to travel, lay out all your clothes and all your money. Then take half the clothes and twice the money."

– Susan Heller

IN THIS CHAPTER

Neato! Nebo baby flashlight plugs into your vehicle's power supply. Never needs batteries. Amazon.com

What to Pack

When it comes to glamping, preparation is paramount, my dear.

A well-equipped wanderer travels in style and comfort—dare I say she's a pampered glamper?

After all, who wants to end up crouching beside a campfire with no tussock for the tushie, or—heaven forbid—no marshmallows for roasting? Not this glamporous girl; I want the works. That's the beauty of trailer traveling: you can pack the essentials *and* the extras.

So, let's get it all out on the table. I'll share my own list of nomadic necessities (as well as little luxuries I love like an ironing-board "table"; umbrellas for shade; a hostess apron; pretty linens; and bling, of course). Use it, own it, and add to it as you wish. It will be your passport to pampering.

Camp Basics ✔ List

- ☐ Tent
- ☐ Bedding (pillows, blankets, sleeping bag)
- ☐ Sleeping pad (p. 66)
- ☐ Multi-tool or knife
- ☐ Daypack for hiking
- ☐ Collapsible camp stools (p. 104) (with cushions, of course)
- ☐ Flashlights (with extra batteries and bulbs)
- ☐ Lanterns (with mantles, if needed, and extra batteries)
- ☐ Lantern fuel or batteries
- ☐ Water filter or treatment tablets, just in case
- ☐ Fishing gear (and license)

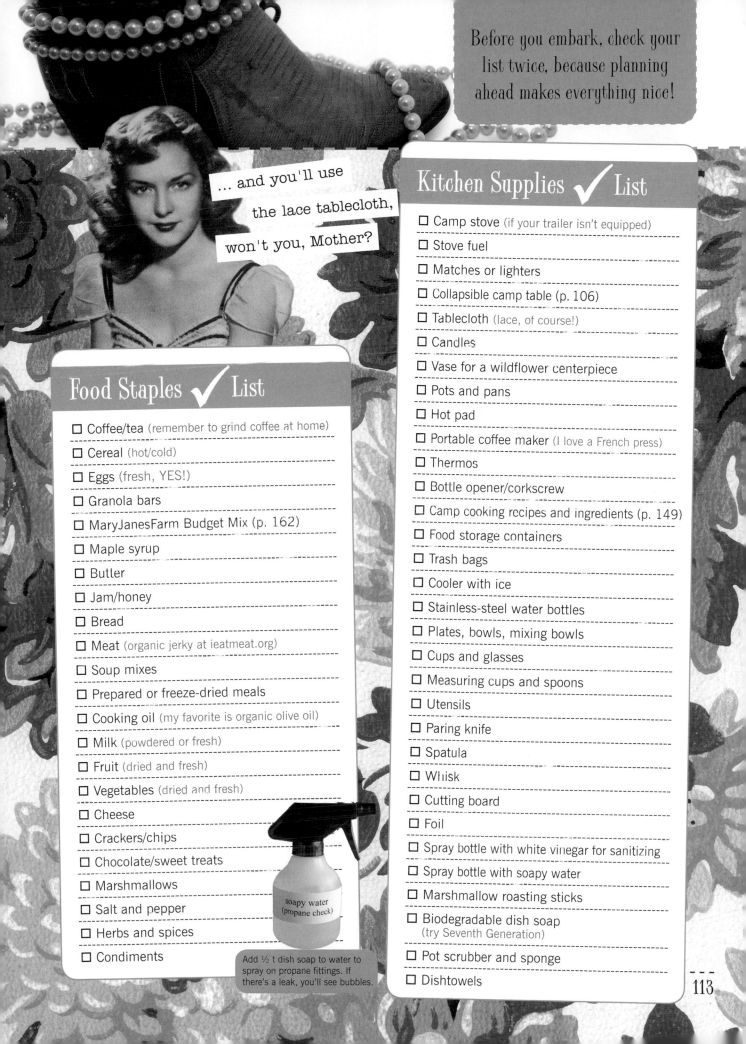

...and you'll use the lace tablecloth, won't you, Mother?

Kitchen Supplies ✓ List

- ☐ Camp stove (if your trailer isn't equipped)
- ☐ Stove fuel
- ☐ Matches or lighters
- ☐ Collapsible camp table (p. 106)
- ☐ Tablecloth (lace, of course!)
- ☐ Candles
- ☐ Vase for a wildflower centerpiece
- ☐ Pots and pans
- ☐ Hot pad
- ☐ Portable coffee maker (I love a French press)
- ☐ Thermos
- ☐ Bottle opener/corkscrew
- ☐ Camp cooking recipes and ingredients (p. 149)
- ☐ Food storage containers
- ☐ Trash bags
- ☐ Cooler with ice
- ☐ Stainless-steel water bottles
- ☐ Plates, bowls, mixing bowls
- ☐ Cups and glasses
- ☐ Measuring cups and spoons
- ☐ Utensils
- ☐ Paring knife
- ☐ Spatula
- ☐ Whisk
- ☐ Cutting board
- ☐ Foil
- ☐ Spray bottle with white vinegar for sanitizing
- ☐ Spray bottle with soapy water
- ☐ Marshmallow roasting sticks
- ☐ Biodegradable dish soap (try Seventh Generation)
- ☐ Pot scrubber and sponge
- ☐ Dishtowels

Food Staples ✓ List

- ☐ Coffee/tea (remember to grind coffee at home)
- ☐ Cereal (hot/cold)
- ☐ Eggs (fresh, YES!)
- ☐ Granola bars
- ☐ MaryJanesFarm Budget Mix (p. 162)
- ☐ Maple syrup
- ☐ Butter
- ☐ Jam/honey
- ☐ Bread
- ☐ Meat (organic jerky at ieatmeat.org)
- ☐ Soup mixes
- ☐ Prepared or freeze-dried meals
- ☐ Cooking oil (my favorite is organic olive oil)
- ☐ Milk (powdered or fresh)
- ☐ Fruit (dried and fresh)
- ☐ Vegetables (dried and fresh)
- ☐ Cheese
- ☐ Crackers/chips
- ☐ Chocolate/sweet treats
- ☐ Marshmallows
- ☐ Salt and pepper
- ☐ Herbs and spices
- ☐ Condiments

soapy water (propane check)

Add ½ t dish soap to water to spray on propane fittings. If there's a leak, you'll see bubbles.

Travel Skirt

It all started with a bonefishing trip to the Yucatán. Carol Louder knew a skirt would be ideal for the climate—and more respectful of the local culture. But it would have to handle the heat and the sun. It couldn't get tangled in her line. It would have to dry quickly after wading. After all that, it would have to stand up to cocktails and dinner. So she made one. Friend Ann Carter pitched in, helping Carol to design a skirt that uses clips and snaps to adjust it to different lengths and styles. They used a rugged, breathable nylon fabric that resists wrinkles, dries quickly, and feels cottony soft. They named it the Macabi Skirt, after the Mayan name for bonefish. MacabiSkirt.com

Pink Goes Fishing

A durable, lightweight fishing vest with 11 pockets to keep your gear organized. Constructed of breathable, ripstop cotton that will feel comfortable even in warm temperatures. LLBean.com

Clothing ✔ List

- ☐ Clothing and footwear for all possible outings and weather changes
- ☐ Sun hat
- ☐ Sunglasses
- ☐ Clothesline and clothespins
- ☐ Laundry bag
- ☐ Laundry soap
- ☐ Clothes washing bag (see p. 83)

100 miles

a hundred miles

100…

Toiletries ✔ List

- ☐ Toilet paper
- ☐ Sunscreen
- ☐ Lip balm
- ☐ Insect repellent (try EcoSmart Organic Insect Repellent)
- ☐ Hand sanitizer (white vinegar works wonders)
- ☐ Mirror
- ☐ Medications as needed
- ☐ Feminine protection
- ☐ GoGirl or Freshette Female Urination Device (see p. 78) (Go-Girl.com)
- ☐ Toothbrush and toothpaste
- ☐ Deodorant (try Tom's)
- ☐ Brush and comb
- ☐ Hair bands/barrettes/bobby pins
- ☐ Biodegradable soap (try Dr. Bronner's)
- ☐ Portable shower (see p. 83)
- ☐ Hand and bath towels
- ☐ Fragrance-free wipes

Extras ✔ List

- ☐ Cell phone (and portable charger)
- ☐ GPS (see p. 145)
- ☐ Tool kit (see p. 119)
- ☐ Preparedness kit (see p. 120)
- ☐ Laptop (with spare battery)
- ☐ Camera (with spare batteries)
- ☐ Binoculars
- ☐ Zip ties
- ☐ Maps and guide books
- ☐ Field guides (flowers, birds, wildlife, etc.)
- ☐ Star chart (try the Star Chart astronomy app from Google Play)
- ☐ Books/magazines
- ☐ Music CDs
- ☐ Notebook and pen
- ☐ Travel alarm clock
- ☐ Umbrella
- ☐ Playing cards
- ☐ Kite

Kanteen To Go
I never leave home without my cute, pink water bottle. Every Klean Kanteen is made from 100% recyclable, high-quality, food-grade stainless steel that's contaminant- and BPA-free. KleanKanteen.com

Glass Act
Lifefactory makes glass water bottles that are BPA-, phthalates-, and PVC-free. LifeFactory.com

It's the little things girls love

Be in Charge!
When it comes to taking a leak, guys have it easy: just aim and fire. No cold buns. No splatter factor. With this handy Sani-Fem Freshette "urinary director," women are now in charge. This lightweight, palm-sized device is reusable and comes with a carrying case. For more information, see p. 78.

Rapid Wash
Fragrance-free wipes from Nature Babycare are an allergen-free way to wash your face. Naty.com

You CAN Take It with You
Make your own glam-travel suitcase ensemble by decoupaging and adding embellishments.

Toolin' Down the Road

Basic Tools and How to Use Them

Out with the Old

There you are, cruising down the open road. Can't you just see the horizon ahead? The world is your oyster, the sunset awaits, your happy little home-on-the-go is trailing along placidly behind you, and then …

KLUNK!

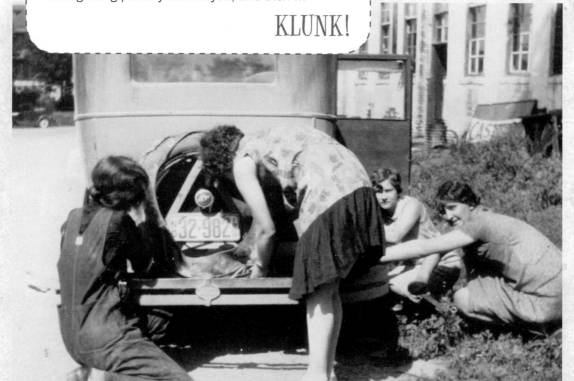

followed by thumpity-thump, thumpity-thump …

Good golly, Miss Molly—

what are you going to do now? Nervously, you pull over onto the shoulder of the conspicuously empty highway. Your knuckles are flashing white on the steering wheel as you peer into the rearview mirror. No! Just as you'd feared—a flat tire. Perhaps you should hunker down and wait. Eventually, you might be able to flag down another driver for help, right? Shudder. That's how women disappear. Okay, so maybe you should call a tow truck. How long will that take? You could be camping precariously alongside the Interstate for hours. At this point, crying is the easiest option. Darn the men in your life for never telling you exactly how to use that, um, tire-changer "thingie"!

In With the New

Dry your eyes, girls. We're leaving the days of distressed damselhood in the dust. Any woman who has the spunk to get out on her own also has every ability to fix a flat—or most other mechanical mishaps that may befall her. All she needs is a nifty set of tools and a smidgen of know-how. Get ready to come to your own rescue.

You've heard this before, but make sure you do a dry run for a flat tire before you actually have one to make sure you have all the right tools.

Get Friendly with Your Owner's Manual

I'll bet your copy is stowed away in the glove compartment of your vehicle, and it may never have been opened. But, your owner's manual can be a fabulous friend when something goes awry on the road.

You don't need to study it from cover-to-cover, but it's important to know that it's available in a hurry. Whether your mishap is minor (you forget how to set your car clock) or major (your dash lights warn that your engine is overheating), your owner's manual will point you toward a can-do solution.

For details on how to change a tire, see p. 142.

woman fixing car©H. Armstrong Roberts/Retrofile/Getty Images

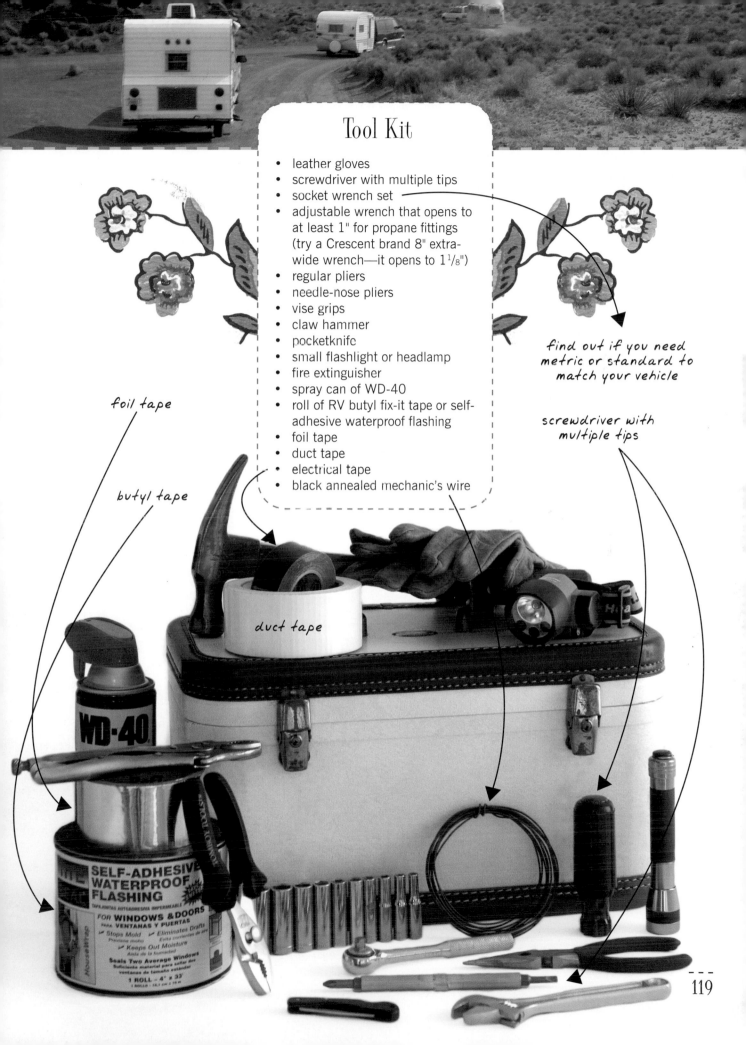

Tool Kit

- leather gloves
- screwdriver with multiple tips
- socket wrench set
- adjustable wrench that opens to at least 1" for propane fittings (try a Crescent brand 8" extra-wide wrench—it opens to $1^{1}/_{8}$")
- regular pliers
- needle-nose pliers
- vise grips
- claw hammer
- pocketknife
- small flashlight or headlamp
- fire extinguisher
- spray can of WD-40
- roll of RV butyl fix-it tape or self-adhesive waterproof flashing
- foil tape
- duct tape
- electrical tape
- black annealed mechanic's wire

find out if you need metric or standard to match your vehicle

screwdriver with multiple tips

foil tape

butyl tape

duct tape

Emergency Preparedness Kit

first-aid kit

magnesium fire starter

round vintage hat box for jumper cables and rope

matches

fire extinguisher

tire chains

hand-crank charger fits any device that has a car power adapter (like a cell phone or camera).

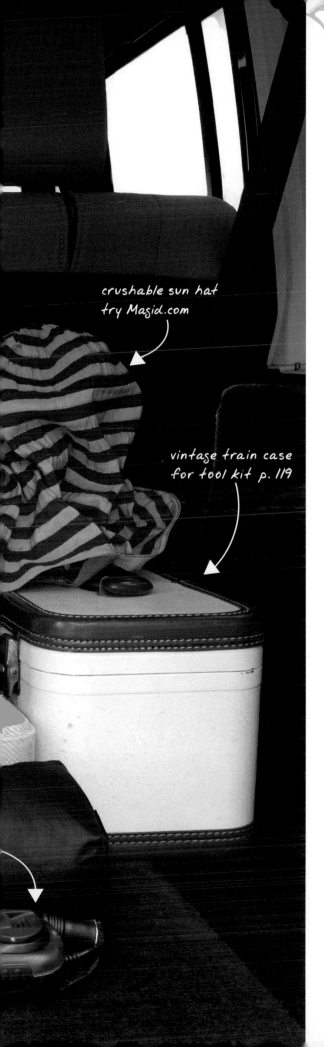

crushable sun hat
try Magid.com

vintage train case
for tool kit p. 119

- Freeplay Eco-Charge hand-crank charger is for use far from outlets. But make sure you have a car power adapter for the devices you want to charge. Also water resistant and compact.
- Garrity hand-crank flashlight
- shovel (I have a Gerber Gorge folding shovel.)
- windshield scraper
- pocketknife
- jumper cables
- rope (good for junktiquing)
- tow rope
- tire chains (Not just for winter. Mine got me out of a mud hole once.)
- emergency flare
- fire extinguisher
- first-aid kit
- insect repellent
- whistle
- 100-hour candle (BePrepared.com)
- matches in waterproof container
- fire starter
- full change of clothes (including a warm pair of socks)
- down parka
- rain poncho (Buy a bright one so it doubles as a flag or help sign.)
- crushable sun hat
- stainless-steel, reusable water bottle
- 1-gallon water (Nalgene makes a collapsible water bottle.)
- water-purification tablets
- non-perishable snack food (I have organic beef jerky in my kit.)
- toilet paper
- busy work (A book, deck of cards, paper and pens, or a knitting project will help keep you occupied and calm during an emergency.)

It doesn't look like it, but the contents of my emergency preparedness kit really do fit into one cute vintage suitcase.

Sleeping Bag under the Stars

Shhhh ...

Night is arching softly across the sky, sprinkling stars like diamond dust as she glides toward the setting sun.

FOR THE FIRST TIME...
Rayon plus Nylon

Stardust
Miracle Slip

never sags
twists *or*
rides up

Lovely JUDY TYLER,
voted Miss Stardust of '49.

The clamor of the day is hushed, a moment of silence, as if every living thing is waiting in reverence for light's mysterious transformation into deep and velvety darkness.

This is a time of magic, and you shiver with awe.

When the pines exhale the cool breath of a breeze, you know it's time to tuck in. You've already spread your ground cloth and sleeping pad. You unroll your sleeping bag with the

slightest whisper of nylon.

This is it,
you marvel.
My little
cocoon for
the night.

How will it transform you?
Sleeping under the stars, without any
semblance of a roof or walls to fence you
in, is a life-changing experience. There is
a sense of vulnerability, primal and raw,
that floods your soul when you set out
to sleep unsheltered. But if you embrace
this feeling and let yourself "fall up" into
the vastness of the sky overhead, you
will discover a strength of spirit that you
may never have known you had.

never a dull moment

Butters' back yard, brothers, neighbor boys and me, 1958

Not to mention, the view is beautiful beyond words! Why count sheep when you can count stars in the Milky Way? In a matter of hours, you will wake at dawn to the scent of dew and the song of birds, and you will bravely shed the warm comfort of your chrysalis to find that your heart has grown a pair of fresh, shimmering wings.

You're ready to fly into a new day of adventure!

Choosing a Sleeping Bag

I'm an old-fashioned girl, and that makes me a diehard devotee of down insulation. You know, feathers—fabulous bird fluff! I still have the down sleeping bag I made 40 years ago using a Frostline kit. Anyone remember those? To my mind, technology simply hasn't been able to master a synthetic filler that can match the light weight, longevity, and miraculous temperature-regulating ability of down. It's no surprise, though, is it? Nature knows best.

So, when you set out to shop for a down sleeping bag, here are a few details to keep in mind:

- Since you probably won't be sleeping under the stars on frigid nights, you won't need a sleeping bag designed for super-low temperatures (they tend to be bulky and more expensive). Depending on your camping climate, look for "ultra-light" summer bags or those that have a 40°F low limit.
- Since one (minor) downfall of down insulation is that it doesn't perform well when wet, you might want to opt for a waterproof, breathable shell to repel moisture. If the weather forecast looks lovely, you probably won't end up wet, but dew and condensation can leave a bag moist in the morning.
- If the thought of sleeping in a cocoon makes you feel claustrophobic, look for a bag with a stretch fabric or zippered expansion baffle that will add roominess for stretching out in all directions.

get down!

126

Caring for Your "Chrysalis"

- Stuff sacks are only created for compacting sleeping bags while traveling. For long-term storage, avoid compression in order to extend the life of your bag. Hang it up in a closet or tuck it loosely into a storage sack or box.
- Down sleeping bags don't like to be washed frequently, but if you need to launder your bag, learn "How to Wash a Down-Insulated Sleeping Bag or Jacket" at DavidLoome.com, under "Do-It-Yourself."
- Better yet, buy a washable liner for your bag. Try Cocoon Cotton Bag Liner/ Travel Sheet at REI.com. Also great for questionable hotel rooms.

Here's how I glamp with my grandgirls, using down sleeping bags that zip together.

Glamper Wisdom

You can duplicate the warmth of a down sleeping bag by climbing into a plastic garbage bag with several geese.

Safety

"My trailer will come unhitched." This actually happened to a friend of mine when she forgot to secure it.

"I'll have a panic attack when I get my trailer stuck at the end of a dirt road." Practice makes **perfect.**

"My propane tank will blow me to smithereens." LP savvy is yours for the taking. LP stands for liquid propane. See, you're already getting up to speed.

"I'll have a heart attack if I have to back up my trailer in public."
By the time I'm done with you, you'll be doing it in **heels.**

"I'll get lost."
Smile.

"My boss will kill me when I decide never to come back home."
!

"People will stare at me."
Head-turning goes with the territory. Smile and blow 'em a kiss.

"Grizzlies, lions, tigers, and bears. Oh my. Snakes. Spiders!"
Piece of cake. It's the two-legged creeps you want to watch out for.

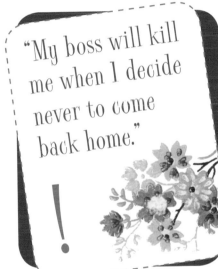

IN THIS CHAPTER

Packing

Heat

Just look at her.

Today's lady-on-the-loose is a vision. With her smartly styled 'do and cropped khakis, she's not afraid to get behind the wheel and go for it. Her trailer is tidy, and her fishing tackle always ready to go. She's a Jane-of-all-trades with a knowing twinkle in her eye. Don't put it past her to fillet a trout and fry it over an open fire without smudging her candy-colored lipstick. She calls the shots. Our highway-bound heroine is proficient. She's poised. She's practically *always* polite. And she's ... packing. That's right, Jane packs a pistol.

Surprised?

If the idea of today's modern woman sporting a sidearm sets you back on your heels, let's talk. I'll be the first to step forward and tell you: I *am* that woman. I love lace, and I wear heels (when I want to). I'm a sucker for glitzy costume jewelry. I can change a tire in a jiffy. And I make marshmallows from scratch to roast over my campfires. These things are true. I also own a handgun. BUT I'm a softie through and through. If I had any say at all, guns would go. Every single one. My persona doesn't *need* a gun, but protecting myself and those I love? Well, at least I can try.

Packing heat doesn't guarantee safety, but it just might help. And in that moment when it does, well, 'nuff said?

The next time you're out and about, stop at the Green Frog Café in Palouse, Washington, where you'll see a homemade apron that I gave them several years ago, being worn by the "man of the house."

deer hunting   Scott, Me, Scottie, and Kent, 1958

How very John Wayne of me, right?

Wrong. In fact, I'm hesitant to even bring the subject up lest you think I'm a-swaggering and a-braggering. I don't like it when guys do that or gals either, for that matter. And I understand why a lot of women are uncomfortable even talking about guns, let alone handling one or owning one. If you didn't grow up with guns like I did, you WILL be uncomfortable. It's a given. But that's the reason for a class or two or three.

Me, Kent, and Scott, 1957

Imagine learning to drive a car for the first time when you're in your 30s or 40s. Cars are dangerous too, but we're just so darn used to them, even though we take our lives into our hands every time we step into a vehicle. And because almost anyone can get behind the wheel of a car, including drunk drivers, your only recourse is to perfect your reaction time, drive defensively, stay alert, and equip yourself with a good car (air bags, etc.), and then ... hope for the best. We all know someone who has been hurt or killed by someone who should never have been given a license to drive, but even that isn't enough to keep us home. I think of guns in the same way. Whether it's a Sunday drive or a night under the stars, the freedom to go where you want to go and be as prepared as you can possibly be is why I'm one of over 15 million women in the U.S. who "pack heat."

It's not a matter of status, but it shouldn't be a subject of secrecy, either.

Don't Jump the Gun

Buying a gun isn't a snap decision, and simply possessing a pistol doesn't guarantee your safety (in fact, it can be downright dangerous). That's why it's important to get gun savvy NOW, before you take to the road or trail and find yourself in trouble. Arm yourself with education and experience, starting with a visit to CorneredCat.com, a fact-packed website created by Kathy Jackson, author of *The Cornered Cat: A Woman's Guide to Concealed Carry.* Kathy's site addresses all aspects of gun ownership, posing questions you may not have known to ask and preparing you to purchase your own pistol. I applied for my concealed weapons permit by taking a class that's offered throughout the U.S. by MyLegalHeat.com. And because I have children afoot, I keep my pistols locked in a variety of tiny safe boxes (both stationary and travel) that only the impression of my unique fingerprint or code can open.

Annie Oakley
at 62 in 1922

Taser C2 Stun Gun

The Odd Thing About Fear

Turning fear into a plan of action can prevent panic. We're more likely to freeze in terror if we can't run through that checklist in our heads we've practiced dozens of times. If a pistol doesn't appeal to you, pepper spray or a stun gun are options you should consider. However, buyer beware. There are stun guns for sale that might even make matters worse. Those cute, tiny, pink guns can't stun through clothing. How likely is it you'll have the opportunity to put it up against someone's neck in order to make direct contact? But, stun guns similar to what police officers use that launch two barbs capable of sending current through clothing can be a more spendy proposition than a pistol. And, like a pistol, they require a background check. Do your homework, girls. I know it's unpleasant to think about all of this, but the odd thing about fear is that ignoring it only makes it stronger. Be aware, prepare, and then get yourself out there!

Finding YOUR Mechanic

His ears perk up at the click-clack sound of heels coming across his concrete floor.

He emerges from under a hoisted Honda, wipes one hand on his gray coveralls and the other through his hair. He calls you, "Ma'am."

You instantly wonder if your pocketbook is about to spring a leak, draining its contents like used motor oil into a mechanic's catch pan.

It's no wonder women dread stepping into a service center. Unless you're familiar with fan belts, fluid levels, and front drive-shafts, you're at a loss as soon as your heels hit the concrete.

As any backwoods survival expert will tell you, "The best way to stay out of trouble is not to get into it."

Whether it's in the wilderness or the auto shop, the rules of survival are the same. So, be willing to take a U-turn, sister, if'n it doesn't feel right. It's easier than you think to ask around beforehand and find YOUR mechanic.

A "Do Right" Mechanic

Start your search for a trusted mechanic online at AskPatty. com, a safe and reliable source for expert automotive advice and research. Not only can you track down answers to common car questions, you can search a directory of "Certified Female Friendly" auto dealers, tire dealers, collision centers, and service departments. Businesses that pass the AskPatty program are experts on how to attract, sell to, retain, and increase loyalty with women customers. Finding a good mechanic is like finding a good pair of shoes ... you might have to try on a few before you find one that fits just right.

"A male gynecologist is like an auto mechanic who has never owned a car."

– Carrie P. Snow

How to Change Your Oil

Handy guy's method:

1. Go to the auto parts store and buy oil, a filter, a container for the dirty used oil, hand cleaner, and maybe a new tool or two.

2. Have a beer to get you inspired.

3. Spend an hour looking for your jack stands. Find them under the Christmas decorations in the back of the garage. Jack up the car.

4. Have another beer to ease your frustration.

5. Place the new drain pan under the car.

6. Look for your $^9/_{16}$" box-end wrench. Give up and use a crescent wrench instead.

7. Unscrew the drain plug.

8. Drop the drain plug in the drain pan, splattering oil onto your head and shirt.

9. Climb out from under the car and use the new hand cleaner on your face. Ignore that tingling sensation.

10. Have another beer.

11. Look for oil-filter wrench. Give up and use a screwdriver to jiggle it out, stabbing your hand in the process.

12. Have another beer to ease the pain.

13. Drag the pan of dirty oil out from under the car, splashing it on the floor in the process.

14. Throw kitty litter on the spill to soak it up.

15. Add new oil to engine. &*#@/!!! Clean up the new oil from the floor and dig the drain plug out of the dirty oil in the drain pan.

16. Walk to the auto parts store to buy more oil.

17. Buy beer.

Smart girl's method:

1. Visit YOUR "do right" mechanic.
2. Drink a cup of coffee. File your nails.
3. Wait 15 minutes. Write a check. Drive off.

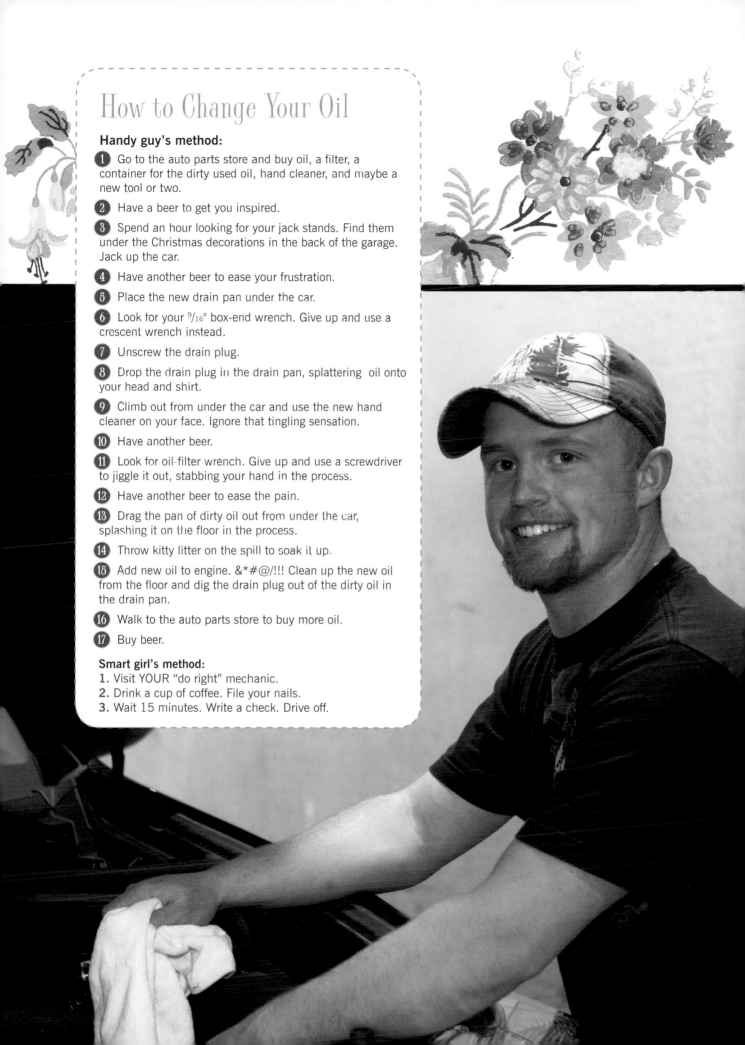

THE WOMAN'S GUIDE TO LOVE AND LASTING RELATIONSHIPS

1. FIND A MAN WHO MAKES YOU LAUGH.

2. FIND A MAN WHO HAS A GOOD JOB AND CAN COOK.

3. FIND A MAN WHO IS HONEST.

4. FIND A MAN WHO WILL PAMPER YOU AND GIVE YOU GIFTS..

5. FIND A MAN WHO IS AWESOME IN THE BEDROOM.

6. MOST OF ALL. IT IS **VERY IMPORTANT** THAT THESE FIVE MEN **NEVER** MEET!

Once you've pinned down a female-friendly prospect, take these steps to make sure the mechanic is right for you:

- Ask the mechanic and/or auto shop to verify certification by the National Institute for Automotive Service Excellence (ASE).
- Check the Better Business Bureau (BBB.org) for complaints on file.
- Ask about warranties for common repairs.
- Do a Web search of the mechanic's name and location in conjunction with words like scam, ripoff, and complaint. If anything major comes up, steer clear.

When you schedule an appointment, remember your rights:

1 You have the authority to approve or reject repairs. When you drop off your car, leave a note with your name, car make and model, and phone number, and set a maximum amount of work the mechanic is authorized to undertake without express permission.

2 You are entitled to a written price estimate for the repairs you have authorized before the work is performed. Generally, this law applies only if you deal face-to-face with the facility and the work is expected to cost more than $100. Once you receive an estimate, the facility may not charge you more than 10% above the estimated costs without your prior approval.

Rascal Flats

Changing a Flat Tire

Don't know where your vehicle's jack is stored? Your owner's manual will tip you off and tell you how to use it, too. In general, here are a few rules of thumb when changing a flat. Remember, tools give leverage—no man muscles required!

1. Before departing on a journey, make sure you have a spare tire that's full of air, a jack, a tire iron (either the jack handle or a separate tool shaped like an "L" or a "T"), and wheel chocks (wedges placed behind the wheels to prevent movement). Tip: Pack a piece of galvanized water pipe about 2' long that fits over the end of your tire iron for extra leverage.

2. If you get a flat, get out your spare, jack, and tire iron and place a wheel chock on the downhill side (even if you're only on a slight incline) of the wheel diagonal to the flat tire to prevent your vehicle from rolling. (If you're towing, chock your trailer as well).

3. If your car has hubcaps, pop them off. If there are no hubcaps, but only caps over each bolt on the rim, pop the caps off with the tip of a screwdriver from your tool kit (p. 119).

4. Fit the tire iron onto one of the lug nuts on the wheel. Turn the tire iron counterclockwise a few turns to loosen the lug nut, but don't remove it. (Repeat after me: "Lefty, Lucy; righty, tighty.") If it's too tight to loosen, use the extender pipe to get more leverage. Then loosen the lug nut opposite the first one and continue working back and forth across the tire until all the nuts are slightly loose.

5. Assemble the jack and position it under the car near the flat tire per the instructions in that trusty owner's manual. Lift the car until the tire is about 1–2" off the ground so that the inflated tire will fit onto the wheel. Safety tip: Never crawl under or put any part of your body under a lifted vehicle or tire.

6. Finish loosening the lug nuts, remove them, and place them where you can reach them and they won't roll away. Pull the tire off and set it aside.

7. Put the spare tire on the wheel with the air valve facing out. Replace the lug nuts, tightening each one by hand in the same manner that you took them off. Then tighten each one using the tire iron in the same pattern, so they seat evenly.

8. Lower the jack to set the car back down, then remove it. Tighten the lug nuts again with the tire iron as tightly as you can. Put any caps or hubcaps back onto the wheel and put your tools and the flat tire into the trunk.

9. Head for the nearest gas station or service center to have your work checked for safety and get your flat repaired.

That being said, the modern girl's solution to a flat tire is to pack a few of those handy "fix a flat" aerosol cans that pump chemical goo into your tire and seal up the hole. You simply inflate the tire with the can and drive to the nearest gas station. When all else fails, call your insurance company for roadside assistance options.

Checking Tire Pressure

If you check the pressure of your tires before leaving home, you probably won't need to worry about checking it again, unless you change altitude dramatically during your trip.

The manufacturer's recommended PSI (Pounds per Square Inch) is printed on the tires as well as in your owner's manual. Your car may also be equipped with a Tire Pressure Monitoring System (TPMS) that will automatically track the pressure and alert you via dashboard signals if you need to add or remove air.

If you want to be a new-fashioned girl, you can buy a digital air pressure gauge.

Even if you have a monitoring system, it's a good idea to have a manual tire gauge at the ready. To use it, simply unscrew the little cap from the valve stem on a wheel, and wiggle the round opening of the tire gauge onto the valve stem. Like magic, a small stick will emerge from the bottom of the tire gauge, telling you the pressure reading for the tire.

If the reading is high compared to the recommended tire pressure, simply use the knob on the backside of the gauge to release air by pushing down partway on the center bead until you hear air coming out. Stop releasing air every few seconds and put the gauge on completely to check the pressure. Do this release/check routine until your tire has the pressure you want.

If the reading is low, go to a gas station and ask if they have an air compressor. Most do, and many are free. Occasionally, it'll cost you a quarter or two for air.

GPS & Google Maps

Remaining Calm While Lost

What is it about men?

Well, okay, we could go on and on about that subject.

Specifically, what is it that cripples men when it comes to asking another human being for directions?

I mean, really, is it so hard?
Stroll into a gas station, question the clerk, then be on your way.
Maybe it's the listening part that challenges them …

Thankfully, today's traveling woman is no longer relegated to the passenger seat, pulling her hair out in frustration when her male companion would rather drive in circles than tuck tail and take someone else's advice.

Modern migration finds Jane behind the wheel, and she has a few tricks up her sleeve.

Not only is she more than capable of asking directions without damaging her pride, she also now has technology at her fingertips that can help her track down the right trail every time—no questions asked.

144

Go Forth and Google

Do you have a destination in mind? If so, make your way to Google.com and click on the "Maps" heading. From there, you can type in practically any location on the planet, and Google will map it for you.

Next, click the "Get Directions" button, and Google will map out the most efficient route for you, from Point "A" to Point "B" with any specified stops in between. You can print the directions and the accompanying map(s) for free.

Globe Trek from Home

One of my favorite aspects of Google mapping is the "Earth" feature. At Google.com/earth, you can download a free software program that lets you "fly" to your destination within seconds. You start out hovering above the globe, and when you type in an address or general region, you *zoom* down to Earth at an exhilarating clip to land in the location of your choice.

Once you land, you can see detailed aerial photos, satellite images, and on-the-ground photos of the area. The best part, though, is that in many places, you can actually dive right into the landscape and explore the images in 3-D, including streets, buildings, and terrain.

For more in-depth adventuring, check out the TUTORIALS page to get help with navigating, searching, touring, adding your own place marks, and more.

Get GPS-Savvy

Don't let the techno-talk freak you out—I'm relatively new to these sorts of electronic gizmos and gadgets myself. But, GPS navigation has helped this homebody globetrot with the best of 'em.

So, what is a GPS?

A GPS (Global Positioning System) unit is a navigational tool that uses satellite signals to pinpoint your latitude and longitude or the location of facilities you're trying to find. These little machines can be mounted in your car or they come portable and pocket-sized.

There are also GPS-capable smart phones that have internal mapping software, and some cell-phone service carriers (AT&T, Sprint, and Verizon) provide GPS navigation that can be accessed wirelessly over the cellular network.

How can a GPS help me find my way?

Once you give it a destination, your GPS can:
- plot your route (shortest, fastest, or most fuel-efficient)
- give spoken, turn-by-turn directions
- show your progress along the route
- alert you to speed warnings
- provide traffic information

Points of interest that a GPS can automatically find for you include:
- gas stations
- ATMs
- campgrounds
- restaurants
- hotels
- tourist attractions

Once you've located your target, a GPS can calculate a route and often provide contact information, should you wish to call ahead.

Voice command is a super-handy feature when you're trying to navigate on the move, allowing you to simply ask your GPS unit for information. Look for peak performance voice command on higher-end models.

Before you shop for a GPS unit, though, learn more about the various models and their capabilities from the GPS Buying Guide at ConsumerReports.org.

Glamping Eats

Don't do it. Don't go "out there" and eat a bunch of junk food.

The formula for getting-away-from-it-all doesn't include tummy upsets. I want you to feel your very best! So I've gathered up some of the playful good food my family and I eat when we're on the road, in our backyard, or entertaining guests. But before you dive in, a word about the ingredients in a few of my recipes. My family and I have been selling organic food mixes, packaged at our farm, for close to 25 years, so no doubt, some of my tried-and-true glamping recipes call for my baking mix (Budget Mix) or gelatin-free gelling agent (ChillOver Powder). I hope I can count on you to give me your vote of confidence. In order to avoid marketing my own products, why would I, in good conscience, recommend gelatin or better-known baking mixes when mine are better for you? If you substitute or improvise, I won't blink an eye, but I ask you to trust my motives. They're as pure as my passion and belief that positive change in the world depends on all of us eating the best food we can get our hands on.

Camp Coffee

Flavored Coffee Creamer

PREP TIME: 10 MINUTES
MAKES: 2¼ CUPS

Mix together:
1   14-oz can sweetened condensed milk
½   cup whole milk
4½   t vanilla extract (or any other desired
combination of extracts or cocoa powder
equaling 4½ t)

Pictured: (top) 3½ t hazelnut extract, 1 t
cinnamon; (middle) 4½ t cocoa powder;
(bottom) 4½ t vanilla extract

Chocolate-Cinnamon Swirl Sticks

Dip cinnamon sticks into melted
chocolate and use to stir coffee.

Chocolate-Covered Espresso Beans

PREP TIME: 10 MINUTES
COOK TIME: 10 MINUTES
MAKES: 16 CANDIES

1   cup dark, milk, or white chocolate chips
1   t creamy peanut butter (to add shine)
16   espresso beans

1. Melt chocolate in the top of a double boiler over medium
heat. Stir in peanut butter until well combined.
2. Fill cavities in a silicone candy mold half full with warm
chocolate. Place an espresso bean in the center of each
cavity. Fill cavities with remaining chocolate. Allow to cool
at room temperature for about 2 hours before unmolding.

Coffee Stir Pops

PREP TIME: 5 MINUTES
COOK TIME: 30–35 MINUTES
MAKES: 26 POPS

1   cup sugar
¾   cup water
½   cup corn syrup
2   t vanilla (or any other desired combination of extracts equaling 2 t)
knot-pick bamboo sticks or popsicle sticks

1. Line a cookie sheet with parchment paper. In a 2-qt saucepan, combine sugar, water, and corn syrup.
2. Bring mixture to a boil over medium heat, whisking frequently. When mixture boils, stop stirring, and boil until mixture reaches 320°F on a candy thermometer (hard-crack stage). Remove from heat.
3. Stir in vanilla. Working quickly, pour candy onto parchment paper 1 t at a time and place a stick into the bottom of each circle.* Allow to cool and dry completely before moving.

*A silicone mold and a funnel with a flow control can help quicken the pouring process so the candy doesn't dry before you can place the sticks.

Pass-Around Appetizers

Sweet & Smoky Zucchini Rolls

PREP TIME: 40 MINUTES
COOK TIME: 10 MINUTES
MAKES: ABOUT 26 ROLLS

7   wooden skewers
½   pineapple, peeled, cored, and cut into ¾" cubes
8   ozs smoked salmon, cut into ¾" squares
2   small zucchini, sliced into ribbons
2   T olive oil
salt and pepper to taste

1. Soak 7 wooden skewers in water for about 20 minutes.
2. Place one piece each of pineapple and salmon at the end of a zucchini ribbon. Roll up and skewer through the pineapple. Repeat for all.
3. Preheat grill to medium heat. Brush rolls with olive oil on all sides and sprinkle with salt and pepper.
4. Cook 4 minutes, flip, and cook for an additional 4 minutes.

Sausage Bites

PREP TIME: 15 MINUTES
COOK TIME: 15 MINUTES
MAKES: FORTY 1" BALLS

2   cups sharp cheddar cheese, grated
½   lb ground hot sausage, uncooked
1½   cups MaryJane's Budget Mix (p. 162)

1. Preheat oven to 400°F.
2. In a large bowl, mix together cheese and sausage.
3. Blend Budget Mix into the cheese and sausage mixture. It will be crumbly.
4. Shape mixture into 1" bite-sized balls.
5. Place balls 1" apart on an ungreased baking sheet; bake for 15 minutes.

Bacon-Wrapped Asparagus

PREP TIME: 15 MINUTES   COOK TIME: 20 MINUTES
MAKES: 12 SPEARS

6   slices bacon
12   large asparagus spears
12   toothpicks

1. Cut bacon in half lengthwise. Wrap bacon strips around spears for one turn to secure, then spiral wrap and secure with toothpicks.
2. Preheat grill and a cast-iron skillet over medium heat. Add spears to skillet and cook, turning, until bacon is crispy.

Potato Salad Pockets

PREP TIME: 20 MINUTES
COOK TIME: 1 HOUR
MAKES: 8 SERVINGS

8   russet potatoes
1   cup mayonnaise
2   celery stalks, diced
2   T apple-cider vinegar
8   bacon slices, cooked until crispy
salt and pepper

1. Preheat oven to 400°F. Scrub potatoes.
2. Bake potatoes until soft in the middle when pierced with a fork, about 1 hour.
3. Cool completely. Slice potatoes in half lengthwise.
4. Using a spoon, scoop out potato pulp, leaving a ½"-thick shell. Transfer pulp to large bowl; add mayonnaise, celery, and vinegar. Crumble bacon and stir into mixture. Season with salt and pepper.
5. Transfer mixture back into potato skins.

Tip: For picnic-perfect pockets, put both sides of the potato back together and secure with a piece of twine.

Casual Cocktail Parties

Banana Cream Pie Cocktail

½ banana, mashed
3 ozs whipped-cream-flavored vodka
4 ozs heavy cream
1½ ozs simple syrup (right)
1 oz lemon juice
whipped cream and cinnamon for garnish

Fill a pint-sized glass to the top with ice. Combine banana, vodka, cream, syrup, and lemon juice and pour over ice. Garnish with whipped cream and a sprinkle of cinnamon.

> " The three-martini lunch is the epitome of American efficiency. Where else can you get an earful, a bellyful, and a snootful at the same time? "
>
> – Gerald Ford

To make lemon twists, you will need a straw and two pins. Cut lemon into thin strips with a lemon zester or a sharp knife. Spiral the lemon strips around the straw, securing each end with a pin.

Happy Glamper

3 ozs lemon juice
10 mint leaves
10 raspberries
1½ t dark brown sugar
2 ozs white rum

Combine lemon juice, mint, raspberries, and sugar in a cocktail shaker (mine is a Mason jar). Muddle until the raspberries are crushed and the mint is fragrant. Add rum and a small handful of ice cubes. Shake for about 2 minutes, until the ice cubes melt a little. Strain into a glass. Garnish with a lemon twist and mint leaves.

Whiskey Sweet & Sour

3 ozs simple syrup (below)
2 ozs whiskey
1 oz lemon juice
orange slice and fresh cherry for garnish

Combine syrup, whiskey, and lemon juice.
Serve over ice or hot. Garnish with orange slice.

Jalapeño Margarita

3 ozs simple syrup (left)
2 ozs tequila
1 oz lime juice
5 jalapeño slices, seeds removed

Combine syrup, tequila, and lime juice.
Pour over ice and add jalapeño slices.

Simple Syrup   MAKES: 1½ CUPS

In a small saucepan, combine 1 cup sugar and 1 cup water.
Heat and stir over medium heat until sugar is dissolved.

Ginger-Sesame Meatballs

PREP TIME: 20 MINUTES
COOK TIME: 18–20 MINUTES
MAKES: 16 MEATBALLS

1 lb lean ground beef
2 T crystallized ginger, minced
1 garlic clove, peeled and minced
2 T honey
½ t salt
½ t sesame oil
1 egg
¼ cup bread crumbs
1 T peanut oil

1. In a medium bowl, combine ground beef, ginger,
garlic, honey, salt, sesame oil, egg, and bread crumbs.
Shape into 16 meatballs.
2. In a skillet over medium heat, fry half of meatballs
in ½ T peanut oil. Repeat for remaining meatballs.

A true glamping gal knows to serve up some yummy nibbles with those cool cocktails.

Ladies Who Brunch

"I haven't trusted polls since I read that 62% of women had affairs during their lunch hour. I've never met a woman in my life who would give up lunch for sex."

– Erma Bombeck

Salmon & Zucchini Kabobs

PREP TIME: 40 MINUTES | COOK TIME: 14–18 MINUTES | MAKES: 12 KABOBS

12	wooden skewers
1¼	lbs salmon, cut into ¾" cubes (about 3 cups)
3	small zucchini, halved and cut into 1" thick slices
½	onion, cut into 1" petals
½	cup white wine
2	sprigs dill, minced
½	t salt
¼	t pepper
1	T olive oil
24	garlic cloves, peeled

1. Soak wooden skewers in water for 20 minutes.
2. In a large bowl, combine salmon, zucchini, onion, wine, dill, salt, pepper, and olive oil.
3. Place a garlic clove at the bottom of each skewer, then layer with zucchini, salmon, onion, ending with a garlic clove.
4. Preheat grill to medium-high and grill skewers for 7–9 minutes on each side.

Easy Scalloped Potatoes

PREP TIME: 25 MINUTES | COOK TIME: 40–45 MINUTES | MAKES: 8 SERVINGS

2½ lbs Yukon Gold potatoes (about 6 medium potatoes), very thinly sliced (¹/₁₆")
1   t salt
1   t pepper
1   cup grated Parmesan cheese
2   cups heavy cream
½   cup cheddar cheese, shredded

1. Lightly butter a cast-iron Dutch oven.
2. Arrange potato slices in a single layer in the bottom of the pan. Sprinkle with about ¼ t salt and ¼ t pepper, then add about ¼ cup grated Parmesan. Continue layering, ending with potatoes.
3. Pour cream over all and top with cheddar.
4. Place Dutch oven on hot coals and arrange several hot coals on top of the Dutch-oven lid (see p. 176). Bake for 40–45 minutes.

Banana-Bread French Toast

PREP TIME: 15 MINUTES | COOK TIME: 20 MINUTES | MAKES: 12 SLICES

3   eggs
¾   cup milk
½   t vanilla extract
¼   t cinnamon

1   T butter
1   loaf banana bread, cut into ¾" slices

1. In a medium bowl, combine eggs, milk, vanilla, and cinnamon.
2. Heat butter on a griddle or in a large skillet over medium heat. Dip banana bread slices into egg mixture. Cook for about 4 minutes on each side, or until golden brown.

Pineapple & Cottage-Cheese Pancakes

PREP TIME: 10 MINUTES | COOK TIME: 10–12 MINUTES | MAKES: 8–9 PANCAKES

1½ cups MaryJane's Budget Mix (p. 162)
2   T sugar
1   egg
½   cup cottage cheese

1½ cups whole milk
1   15-oz can pineapple slices, drained

1. In a medium bowl, combine Budget Mix and sugar.
2. In a separate bowl, whisk together egg, cottage cheese, and milk.
3. Add wet mixture to the dry mixture and stir just until blended.
4. Lightly oil a griddle or large skillet and heat over medium-low heat. Place a pineapple ring on the pan and cover with pancake batter. Repeat, leaving ample space between pancakes. Flip pancakes after bubbles form and edges have lost their sheen.

Potlucks

Camp Chipotle Chili

PREP TIME: 20 MINUTES   COOK TIME: 35–40 MINUTES
MAKES: 8 SERVINGS

2	lbs lean ground beef
1	red onion, peeled and diced
1	yellow pepper, seeded and diced
2	14-oz cans black beans, drained
1	14.5-oz can fire-roasted tomatoes, drained
2	14-oz cans tomato sauce
1	chipotle pepper, finely minced
2	T adobo sauce
½	t salt
2	t brown sugar
½	cup cilantro leaves, minced
1	avocado, diced
sour cream	

1. Brown beef in a Dutch oven; drain. Add onion and yellow pepper and cook over moderate heat for 5 minutes.
2. Stir in beans, tomatoes, tomato sauce, chipotle pepper, adobo sauce, salt, and brown sugar. Simmer over moderate heat for about 20 minutes.
3. Add cilantro. Serve with avocado and sour cream.

Cantaloupe & Cucumber Salad

PREP TIME: 15 MINUTES
MAKES: ABOUT 12 CUPS

1	small cantaloupe (about 3 lbs), peeled, seeded and cut into 1" pieces
2	English cucumbers, partially peeled, quartered, and sliced
½	cup mint leaves, minced
¼	cup honey
2	T white wine vinegar

1. In a large bowl, combine cantaloupe, cucumber, and mint leaves.
2. In a small bowl, whisk together honey and vinegar. Pour over cantaloupe mixture and stir well.

Mac & Cheese

PREP TIME: 30 MINUTES
COOK TIME: 45-50 MINUTES
MAKES: 12 SERVINGS

- 1 lb macaroni
- 3 T butter
- 1 yellow onion, peeled and thinly sliced
- 1 t salt
- 6 cups grated Colby-jack cheese
- 3 cups milk

1. In a large pot, cook pasta for 7–9 minutes in 6 cups of boiling water.
2. While pasta is cooking, melt butter in a large skillet and add onion. Cook for about 8 minutes, stirring occasionally. Drain pasta and stir in salt and cheese.
3. Transfer half of pasta mixture to a Dutch oven and layer half of the onion, then remaining pasta mixture. Pour milk over all and top with remaining onion.
4. Place Dutch oven on hot coals and arrange several hot coals on top of the Dutch-oven lid (see p. 176). Bake for 45–50 minutes.

Zucchini Lattice Tart

PREP TIME: 50 MINUTES, PLUS 1 HOUR CHILLING
COOK TIME: 30 MINUTES   MAKES: 12 SERVINGS

Crust:
- 2½ cups flour
- ½ t salt
- 12 T butter
- ⅓ cup cold water
- 1 egg yolk

Filling:
- ½ cup cheddar cheese
- ¾ lb hot Italian sausage, cooked and drained
- ¾ cup feta cheese
- 1 yellow squash, cut into ribbons
- 1 zucchini, cut into ribbons
- salt

1. In a medium bowl, combine flour and salt. Using a pastry blender, cut in butter until mixture resembles coarse crumbs.
2. In a small bowl, combine water and egg yolk. Mix into flour and stir until dough forms. Shape dough into a disk, wrap in plastic wrap, and refrigerate for 1 hour.
3. Preheat oven to 400°F. Roll dough out on a lightly floured surface. Transfer dough to a 9" square pan and form edges. Line crust with foil and weigh down with pie weights or dry beans. Bake for 10 minutes.
4. Remove pie weights or beans, sprinkle cheddar over bottom of the tart, layer sausage, and top with feta.
5. Arrange yellow squash and zucchini in a lattice pattern on top and salt to taste. Bake for 20 minutes.

Picnic Fare

Watermelon Salsa

PREP TIME: 20 MINUTES
MAKES: ABOUT 4 CUPS

1	small seedless watermelon (about 3 lbs), peeled and cut into ¼" pieces
½	t salt
2	cups pineapple, cut into ¼" pieces
½	cup cilantro leaves, minced
1	shallot, peeled and minced
¼	t red pepper flakes
2	T white balsamic vinegar

1. Place a colander over a bowl, and pour cut watermelon into the colander. Mix in salt. Let watermelon drain for 10 minutes.
2. Meanwhile, in a medium bowl, combine remaining ingredients. Stir in watermelon. Serve with tortilla chips.

BLT Salad

PREP TIME: 20 MINUTES
COOK TIME: 15 MINUTES
MAKES: ABOUT 6 CUPS

1	lb bacon, cooked and diced
4	cups shredded napa cabbage
½	avocado, diced
1½	cups grape tomatoes, quartered
¼	t pepper
½	cup mayonnaise

1. Combine all ingredients in a medium bowl.
Serve on sandwich rolls.

Don't forget to bring plenty of water to your picnic. Put small containers of water in the freezer for a few hours before—they'll do double duty to keep your picnic hamper cold.

Peanut Butter Buddies

PREP TIME: 10 MINUTES
MAKES: 3 SERVINGS
A protein-packed, crustless snack-on-the-go.

12	2–3" rounds sliced bread
¼	cup peanut butter
¼	cup raisins
¼	cup peanuts, chopped

1. Spread peanut butter on 6 slices of bread.
Sprinkle with raisins and peanuts. Top with
rest of bread rounds.

Nibbles & Snacks

Bread Sticks

PREP TIME: 15 MINUTES
COOK TIME: 15 MINUTES
MAKES: 20 BREAD STICKS

2	cups MaryJane's Budget Mix (right)
3	T cold butter, cut into ½" pieces
⅔	cup buttermilk
2	T olive oil
¼	cup fresh herbs, chopped (thyme, rosemary, basil, dill, etc.)
¼	cup Parmesan cheese, grated

order online:
MaryJanesFarm.org
(also available gluten-free)

1. Preheat oven to 400°F.
2. In a medium bowl, cut butter into Budget Mix. Stir in buttermilk to form dough.
3. Turn onto a floured board and form into a ¼"-thick rectangle. Brush top with oil and sprinkle with herbs and cheese. Cut into 1"-wide strips, twist, and place on an ungreased baking sheet. Press ends of bread sticks to pan to prevent shrinkage.
4. Bake for 15 minutes or until golden brown. Serve with marinara for dipping.

Parmesan Crisps

PREP TIME: 8 MINUTES   COOK TIME: 5–7 MINUTES   MAKES: 18 CRISPS

1   cup shredded Parmesan cheese
salt and pepper

1. Preheat oven to 400°F. Line two cookie sheets with parchment paper.
2. Spoon 2 t Parmesan onto cookie sheets and spread into 2" circles, leaving about 1" of space between each crisp. Sprinkle with salt and pepper.
3. Bake for 5–7 minutes, or until Parmesan is golden brown. Remove from oven and let cool for 5 minutes. Transfer to a cooling rack and cool completely.

Cinnamon Toast to Go

PREP TIME: 15 MINUTES   COOK TIME: 20–23 MINUTES
MAKES: 8 CUPS

8   cups ¾" bread cubes
¼   t nutmeg
1½   t cinnamon
¼   cup sugar
4   T butter, melted

1. Preheat oven to 425°F. In a large bowl, combine all ingredients. Toss until bread cubes are evenly coated.
2. Spread bread cubes onto a cookie sheet in a single layer. Bake for 20–23 minutes, or until golden brown and crispy.

Mustard Pretzel Sheets

PREP TIME: 15 MINUTES   COOK TIME: 15 MINUTES   MAKES: 2 SHEETS

3   T olive oil, divided
1½   cups MaryJane's Budget Mix (left)
¼   t salt
¾   cup buttermilk

1   t baking soda
3   T water
2   t dry mustard
     stone-ground mustard

1. Preheat oven to 450°F. Brush two cookie sheets with ½ T olive oil each. In a medium bowl, combine Budget Mix, salt, remaining 2 T olive oil, and buttermilk.
2. Roll dough out on a floured surface into a large rectangle (roughly the size of 2 cookie sheets) cut in half, and place halves on cookie sheets.
3. In a small bowl, combine baking soda and water. Brush half the baking soda mixture over the surface of the dough. Sprinkle dry mustard evenly on top.
4. Bake for 12 minutes. Brush with remaining water/baking soda mix, and bake for an additional 3 minutes, or until sheets are a deep, golden brown. Cool and break into pieces. Serve with stone-ground mustard.

Roasted Chickpeas

PREP TIME: 40 MINUTES   COOK TIME: 40 MINUTES   MAKES: 2 CUPS

1   29-oz can chickpeas
3   T grated Parmesan cheese
1   T parsley, minced

½   t salt
2   T olive oil

1. Preheat oven to 400°F. Drain and rinse chickpeas, spread out in a single layer on a cookie sheet, and let dry for about 5 minutes. Remove and discard outer skins.
2. In a medium bowl, combine all ingredients and toss to coat.
3. Spread chickpeas onto a cookie sheet in a single layer. Roast for about 40 minutes, stirring occasionally.

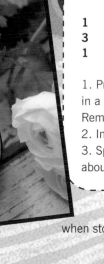

Note: All these nibbles and snacks can pick up moisture when stored; keep as dry as possible, preferably in the open air unless humid.

Grilled Corn with Cilantro-Lime Butter

PREP TIME: 20 MINUTES
COOK TIME: 10 MINUTES
MAKES: 8 SERVINGS

½ cup unsalted butter, softened
3 cups fresh cilantro, finely chopped
1 T fresh lime juice
1 t sea salt
8 ears fresh corn on the cob
olive oil

1. In a small bowl, mash together the butter, cilantro, lime juice, and salt. Form into a log shape and roll in plastic wrap. Refrigerate for several hours, until firm.
2. Shuck the corn and trim ends. Soak corn in a pot of cold, salted water for 10 minutes.
3. Light the coals or preheat the grill to medium heat. Brush grill grate lightly with oil.
4. Place corn on grill and turn every 2–3 minutes, for a total of 10 minutes. Remove corn from grill and top each ear with a slice (1 T) of cilantro butter.

Grilled Potato Salads

Here's a great way to make summer potato salads. Bake the potatoes ahead of time as you normally would, but remove them from the oven while they're slightly al dente. Allow to cool completely, then throw them in your cooler. When you're ready to make a salad, cut the potatoes into ¾" cubes, skins and all, then skewer them. Brush generously with olive oil and sprinkle with salt and pepper. Place skewers on your grill and cook, turning frequently, until potatoes are golden brown and crispy, then add them to one of the following recipes while still warm.

Smoked Bacon & Mustard Salad
(6 SERVINGS)

3   small shallots, peeled and finely diced
3   T olive oil
3   T whole-grain mustard
2   T red-wine vinegar
½   t salt
freshly cracked pepper
6   cups grilled potatoes (above)
3   slices smoked bacon, cooked and crumbled
3   T fresh parsley, minced

Sauté shallots in olive oil until barely softened; remove from heat and add mustard, vinegar, salt, and pepper. Toss with warm potatoes, bacon, and parsley.

- -

Fennel & Chimichurri Salad
(6 SERVINGS)

(Chimichurri is a slightly spicy South American condiment made from oil, vinegar, and fresh herbs.)

1   bulb fennel, thinly sliced
⅓   cup Chimichurri Sauce (below)
6   cups grilled potatoes (above)

Toss fennel and sauce with warm potatoes.

Chimichurri Sauce (1½ CUPS)
¼   cup onion, peeled and finely diced
½   cup parsley, minced
3   T cilantro, minced
3   garlic cloves, peeled and minced
½   t ground cumin
½   t crushed red pepper
½   cup olive oil
¼   cup red-wine vinegar
½   t salt
¼   t pepper

Mix all ingredients and let stand for 2 hours.

Greek Salad (ABOVE, 6 SERVINGS)
⅔   cup plain yogurt
⅓   cup sour cream
⅓   cup finely grated cucumber
      (squeeze to remove liquid)
1   garlic clove, peeled and minced
1   cup tomatoes, seeded and diced
1   cup cucumber, peeled, seeded, and diced
1   cup black olives, sliced
1   cup feta cheese, crumbled
6   cups grilled potatoes (above)
salt and pepper to taste

Mix together yogurt, sour cream, cucumber, and garlic. Combine remaining ingredients, toss with warm potatoes, and gently fold in yogurt sauce.

- -

Southwestern Salad (6 SERVINGS)
1   cup fresh corn, cooked, and cut from cob
1   roasted red pepper, diced
¼   cup red onion, peeled and finely diced
2   garlic cloves, peeled and minced
2   T cilantro, minced
2   T olive oil
2   T red wine vinegar
½   t salt
freshly cracked pepper
6   cups grilled potatoes (above)

Toss all ingredients with warm potatoes.

Onion Cup Mini-Meatloaves

PREP TIME: 20 MINUTES
COOK TIME: 35–40 MINUTES
MAKES: 6 SERVINGS

3	red onions, peeled	juice of ½	lemon
1	lb lean ground beef	½	t salt
¼	cup minced chives	1	egg
2	T dill, minced	⅔	cup bread crumbs
½	cup sour cream	2	t olive oil for brushing

1. Cut onions in half lengthwise and remove centers, leaving 3–4 layers of the onion for a cup.
2. In a medium bowl, combine ground beef, chives, dill, sour cream, lemon juice, salt, egg, and bread crumbs. Divide mixture into 6 equal portions and place in onion cups. Brush tops of meatloaves with oil and wrap each meatloaf generously in foil.
3. Preheat grill to medium heat and cook for about 20 minutes on each side. Garnish with sour cream and chives.

No-Fuss Kabobs

PREP TIME: 30 MINUTES   COOK TIME: 10 MINUTES   MAKES: 6 KABOBS

Rather than assembling these kabobs and then barbecuing them, this reverse approach ensures that the wooden skewers stay intact for easier handling.

1	large red pepper, cut in half and seeded	2	T olive oil
6	large mushrooms	6	small white onions
3	smoked sausage links		stone-ground mustard
			wooden skewers

1. Preheat grill to medium-high heat.
2. Brush pepper, mushrooms, and sausages with oil. Grill until pepper and sausages are slightly charred and mushrooms have softened. Remove and cool.
3. Cut sausages into 1" pieces. Cut pepper into bite-size chunks and mushrooms in half.
4. Assemble kabobs, alternating peppers, mushrooms, and sausages, and ending with an onion.
5. Serve cold or at room temperature with hearty mustard.

" Give a gal a barbecue, feed her for a day; teach a gal to barbecue, and feed her for the summer. "

Use a "charcoal chimney" instead of liquid starter to light your coals. It's a metal cylinder with a charcoal grate mounted inside. You pop unlit charcoal up top and newspaper underneath and light it. The newspaper burns and lights the charcoal on top, using a "chimney effect." Then, just dump the coals onto the grill and you're ready to barbeque. Find charcoal chimneys in your local hardware or department store.

Grilled Brown-Sugar Bananas

PREP TIME: 10 MINUTES
COOK TIME: 5–6 MINUTES
MAKES: 4 SERVINGS

safflower oil
2   firm bananas
juice of ½ lemon
¼   cup brown sugar
¼   t cinnamon
ice cream (try coconut ice cream)

1. Preheat grill to medium heat. Brush grill grate lightly with oil.
2. With peel intact, cut each banana in half lengthwise. Brush cut side with lemon juice.
3. In a large bowl, combine sugar and cinnamon. Coat the cut side of each banana half with the sugar mixture.
4. Place bananas on the grill, cut side down. Grill for 2–3 minutes per side. Remove from grill and allow to cool for a few minutes. Peel bananas and serve in bowls, cut side up, with your favorite ice cream. (Or go all-out and make banana splits with chocolate syrup, whipped cream, and walnuts!)

Hot idea! Grill your favorite fruit like pineapple, mangoes, watermelon, strawberries, or peaches, drizzle with balsamic vinegar, and top with chopped mint. Grilling intensifies the sweetness of fruit since it caramelizes the natural sugars. Balsamic vinegar's sweet-tart flavor pairs nicely with grilled fruit.

I pack a Weber Go-Anywhere Grill in my teardrop. But the small propane bottles don't have enough pressure—bring along a large tank and an adaptor hose.

Grilled Pineapple-Rum Skewers

PREP TIME: 20 MINUTES
COOK TIME: 10 MINUTES
MAKES: 4 SERVINGS

wooden skewers
safflower oil
½   cup rum
½   cup brown sugar
½   t vanilla extract
¼   t ground cinnamon
1   large pineapple, peeled, cored, and cut into 1½" cubes
vanilla-bean ice cream

1. Soak wooden skewers in water for 20 minutes.
2. In the meantime, preheat grill to medium heat. Brush grill grate lightly with oil.
3. In a small bowl, mix rum, sugar, vanilla, and cinnamon together until sugar is dissolved.
4. In a large bowl, combine rum mixture and pineapple and coat well. Let stand for 5 minutes.
5. Skewer pineapple and place on grill. Reserve rum mixture. Grill for 10 minutes, turning occasionally. Remove from grill and let pineapple cool for 5 minutes; remove fruit from skewers. Serve in bowls with a scoop of ice cream and drizzle remaining rum-sugar mixture on top.

Campfire Cooking

The Never-Fail Campfire

Nothing is cozier than snuggling up beside a crackling fire on a cool, starry evening, but we tend to defer to our male counterparts when it comes to fire building. Well, ladies, it's time to get in touch with your inner Goddess of Flame. The secret to fire lighting is surprisingly simple, so get sizzling!

Chimeneas and fire bowls are good alternatives if you don't have a place for an outdoor fire pit. Chimeneas are portable outdoor fireplaces made of terra-cotta, steel, or copper. Spark screens and a fireproof mat are a must if using a chimenea on a wooden deck or patio. Fire bowls (or pits) are made of metal and come in a variety of finishes and decorative designs. Some are as simple as a bowl with legs, while others are enclosed with glass or screens to contain flying sparks. Fire bowls were traditionally used for burning small pieces of wood, but they can also be fitted with alternative fuel sources such as gas, gel alcohol, or charcoal.

> **To poke a wood fire** is more solid enjoyment than almost anything else in the world.
> – Charles Dudley Warner

How to Create Sparks and Lasting Flames:

1. Build a small pile of paper balls (newspapers or brown paper bags) and arrange a pyramid of small dry sticks (about a gallon bucket's worth) around it, making sure there is plenty of air space.
2. Light the paper.
3. When the small sticks start to catch fire, start adding slightly larger pieces of wood in pyramid formation (a typical bundle of split, dry firewood that you can carry in your arms will sustain a small campfire for up to 2 hours). If you have difficulty lighting the fire, dismantle it and start over.
4. Once your fire is going strong, you can add logs as needed, leaving air spaces in between. Never leave a fire unattended. When you're ready to put the fire out, let it burn down as much as possible, then douse it with water and stir with a stick until the coals and ashes are cool to the touch.

Dry pine needles are one of nature's best fire starters.

Glamper Wisdom

Lint from your navel makes a handy fire starter. Warning: Remove lint from navel before lighting.

Homemade Fire Starters

Stuff dryer lint (from cottons only, no synthetics) into the compartments of an empty cardboard egg carton, then pour melted wax from all the little bits of leftover candles you've been saving over your lint "eggs," and you'll be hatching a fire whenever you need one.

Cooking with Cast Iron

Cast iron makes me feel nostalgic. Just the sight of a well-seasoned skillet conjures up images of hearty women in long-ago kitchens who understood the vital essence of home cooking. Our grandmothers were some of these women, and their mothers before them. I've heard that George Washington's mother so revered her cast-iron cookware that she made special note of it in her will. Actually, cast iron dates all the way back to ancient China, where blast furnaces were first developed to heat and melt iron for molding. All these years later, people keep returning to cast iron because its attributes are timeless. It heats evenly. It moves seamlessly from stovetop to oven to campfire. Unlike aluminum, copper, and stainless steel, cast iron doesn't leach harmful metals or chemicals into your food (it does release traces of iron, but they're not dangerous and may even contribute a bit of beneficial iron to your diet). Plus, with proper care, cast iron will last lifetimes. Just imagine the luscious mealtime memories one pan might pass from generation to generation.

Who doesn't love a campfire meal?

I contend people bond better without a roof over their heads, and I'm always on the lookout for dinners that get everyone involved. Pie irons allow each person to make and bake her own meal. But don't let the "pie" part of these cast-iron devices mislead you. For under $20 each, you can buy waffle, dog 'n' brat, bread 'n' biscuit, panini, round hamburger (I use it to roast chicken breasts), and even square "just about anything including toasted pecans" pie irons for your evening escapades. Try Amazon.com.

Resurrect a Beyond-Hope, Rusty Cast-Iron Skillet

When you shop for cast iron, don't overlook used cookware at garage sales and flea markets. Old cast iron—even rusty cast iron—can be coaxed back to life with a little TLC.

What you do need to look for in terms of cooking quality:

- Surface texture should be uniformly rough (like a cat's tongue). Avoid pieces that are pitted, chipped, cracked, warped, or deeply scratched.
- The thickness of the iron should be the same all the way around.
- Ideally, buy American-made because of safety standards which regulate the materials and manufacturing process.

Use a drill with a coarse 2" crimped, wire-cup brush bit to remove corrosion. Go over the surface with fine-grit sandpaper. Then wash the pan in hot, soapy water. (Use soap this one time only because once your pan is seasoned, you don't want the soap to break down the lovely smooth "cure" you're about to create.) Rinse and dry completely. Preheat your oven to 350°F. Now rub a thin layer of oil over the iron, both inside and outside the pan. Organic shortening works like a charm. Good quality, salt-free lard works also. Once it's oiled up, place the pan upside down on the top shelf of the oven so the oil doesn't pool up in the pan. Place a baking sheet on the bottom shelf to catch any drips. Bake for one hour, then turn the oven off and leave the pan inside until it's cool. When you pull it out, the surface will shine.

Be sure to wear safety goggles while working on any project that could result in eye injury. Elvex Safety with Style has a line of safety glasses just for women—smaller, safe, *and* stylish! Elvex.com/safety-glasses-for-women.htm.

Campfire Chicken Salad

PREP TIME: 20 MINUTES
COOK TIME: 15 MINUTES
MAKES: 8 SERVINGS

2   boneless skinless chicken breasts
     (about 2 lbs)
2   cups seedless red grapes, quartered*
2   cups celery (about 8 stalks), diced
2   cups pecans, toasted and finely chopped
1½ cups mayonnaise
1   T sugar
2   T lemon juice
½ t salt
¼ t pepper

1. Grill chicken breasts over hot coals until cooked through. Allow to cool slightly, then finely dice.
2. In a large bowl, combine chicken, grapes, celery, and pecans.
3. In a small bowl, whisk together mayonnaise, sugar, lemon juice, salt, and pepper. Pour over chicken and toss to coat.

*This salad is also delicious with 1 cup of golden raisins in place of the red grapes.

Cast-Iron Waffles

PREP TIME: 10 MINUTES
COOK TIME: 40 MINUTES
MAKES: 5 WAFFLES

1½ cups MaryJane's Budget Mix (p. 162)
2   T sugar
2   large eggs
1½ cups milk

1. In a medium bowl, stir together the Budget Mix and sugar.
2. In a separate bowl, whisk together the eggs and milk.
3. Add liquid ingredients to the budget mixture; stir just until blended with small lumps.
4. Ladle onto a lightly oiled waffle iron.
Cook 3–4 minutes per side.

Tips for better cast-iron waffles:

1. Make sure your waffle iron is well seasoned. Additional oil may be needed between waffles.
2. Make sure your waffle iron is very hot before pouring in batter. You need a good base of coals in the fire, but if it's too hot, the waffles will burn. Never place in open flames.
3. Don't open the iron to peek. You may ruin the waffle, and besides—you're cheating.

Find recipe for Salmon & Zucchini Kabobs on p. 156.

Old-fashioned waffle irons designed for use with wood cook stoves are perfect for campfire cast-iron waffles. Fill the lower compartment with campfire coals. The top part of the waffle iron is designed to swivel and turn above the hot coals for browning both sides.

How to Fillet a Fish

> " Nothing cooks
> fresh-caught fish
> like a cast-iron pan. "

1. After you've gutted the fish, lay it on its side on a cutting board (or a good, flat rock if you're in the outback), and keep it as cool as possible during the fileting process. Using a sharp fillet knife, make the first cut behind the gills, as if you're going to cut off the head. Cut only until the knife touches the backbone (don't cut the head off completely).

2. Insert the knife near the spine and cut gently down the length of the fish from gills to tail, barely touching the ribcage with the underside of your blade while using the backbone as a guide, so that the meat "peels" away from the bones.

3. Continue cutting until you reach the tail. Flip the fish over and repeat on the other side.

4. With each fillet laid skin side down, remove the skin by inserting the knife at the tail end and slicing the meat from the skin.

Tip: My father grew better roses than anyone. He claims it was because he buried fish remains around his bushes (fish fertilizer)!

Butters family fishing: Kent, MaryJane, and Scott, weekend camping, 1958.

Pan-Fried Trout with Mushrooms & Lemon-Cream Sauce

PREP TIME: 15 MINUTES
COOK TIME: 20–25 MINUTES
MAKES: 6 FILLETS

1   cup heavy cream
½   t salt, divided
juice of ½ lemon
4   T butter
6   trout fillets
10 crimini mushrooms, quartered
4   garlic cloves, peeled and minced
⅓   cup parsley leaves, minced
1   T dill, minced
2   t tarragon, minced

1. In a small saucepan, combine cream and ¼ t salt. Bring to a boil over medium heat, reduce heat, and simmer until cream is thickened (about 10–12 minutes), stirring frequently. Add lemon juice. Keep warm.
2. Melt butter on a large griddle over medium coals. Add trout fillets and cook for 4–5 minutes. Flip over; sprinkle with remaining ¼ t salt. Add mushrooms, garlic, parsley, dill, and tarragon. Cook for an additional 4–5 minutes.
3. Remove from heat and pour cream sauce over fish.

Butters family catch of the day, 1950s

Plum Cobbler

PREP TIME: 20 MINUTES
COOK TIME: 45 MINUTES
MAKES: 8 SERVINGS

6	cups Italian prune plums, pitted and quartered
½	cup sugar
¼	cup flour
½	t ground cinnamon
¼	t ground nutmeg
⅛	t salt

Topping:

1	cup flour
3	T stone-ground cornmeal
⅓	cup sugar
1½	t baking powder
¼	t baking soda
¼	t salt
½	cup buttermilk
3	T butter, melted

1. Toss plums with the next five ingredients; place in a cast-iron Dutch oven.
2. In a medium bowl, combine dry topping ingredients.
3. In a small bowl, whisk together buttermilk and butter.
4. Add liquid ingredients to flour mixture; mix well.
5. Drop topping by spoonfuls on top of plum mixture. Cover.
6. Place Dutch oven on hot coals and arrange several hot coals on top of the Dutch-oven lid (left). Bake for about 45 minutes.

Some cast-iron Dutch ovens have a deeply rimmed top lid for holding hot coals to create a campfire "oven" for "baking." If yours has a domed lid, you can put the lid on upside down to hold coals, but you'll have to allow extra room for the lid by filling your pot only ¾ full. Place the pot in hot coals after the fire has died down—never place a pot on open flames. Dutch-oven cooking is an art of its own—there's even an International Dutch Oven Society (IDOS.com).

176

Salmon & Asparagus Dinner

PREP TIME: 10 MINUTES

COOK TIME: 10–20 MINUTES, DEPENDING ON HEAT OF COALS

MAKES: 2 SERVINGS

5	T butter, divided
12	oz salmon
salt and pepper	
½	red onion, peeled and sliced into ¼" half rings
5	garlic cloves
10–12	spears asparagus, sliced lengthwise (snap bottoms off first)
½	bulb fennel, sliced into ¼" half rings, and fronds (optional)
3	slices lemon
2	T heavy cream

Place 2 pats of butter on a sheet of long, heavy-duty foil; top with salmon; lightly salt and pepper salmon. Layer onion, garlic, asparagus, and fennel, if using; lightly salt and pepper vegetables. Top with lemon slices, remaining 3 pats butter, and fennel fronds, if using. Pour cream over top. Bring foil up and around ingredients and seal well. Using more long, heavy-duty foil, wrap package in two more layers. Place packets on hot coals after the fire has died down—never place packets on open flames.

Beef & Potatoes Dinner

PREP TIME: 10 MINUTES

COOK TIME: 10–20 MINUTES, DEPENDING ON HEAT OF COALS

MAKES: 2 SERVINGS

¾	lb ground beef
6	T butter, divided
salt and pepper	
3	medium red potatoes, cut into large cubes
3	carrots, sliced lengthwise
½	onion, peeled and sliced into ¼" half rings
8	mushrooms, halved
5	whole garlic cloves

Place ground beef on a sheet of long, heavy-duty foil; flatten to a 6" square. Top with 3 pats of butter and press into ground beef; lightly salt and pepper meat. Layer potatoes, carrots, onion, mushrooms, and garlic; lightly salt and pepper vegetables. Top with remaining 3 pats butter. Bring foil up and around ingredients and seal well. Using more long, heavy-duty foil, wrap package in two more layers. Place packets on hot coals after the fire has died down—never place packets on open flames.

welder's gloves go hand-in-hand
with campfire cooking

Delish Desserts

Key Lime Pie à Go-Go
PREP TIME: 30 MINUTES
MAKES 10–12 SERVINGS

2   8 oz packages cream cheese
1   14-oz can sweetened condensed milk
½   cup lime juice*
1   box graham crackers

1. Place cream cheese in a food processor and whip. With processor running, add condensed milk and lime juice; mix thoroughly.
2. Spread filling between graham crackers.

*Try different flavors. For cheesecake flavor, mix in 2 T lemon juice, 1 T vanilla, and seeds from 1 vanilla bean in place of the lime juice. For peanut flavor, mix in ⅓ cup peanut butter in place of the lime juice. For blackberry flavor, mix in 2 T lemon juice and ¼ cup blackberries in place of the lime juice.

Campfire Banana Split
PREP TIME: 5 MINUTES
COOK TIME: 5 MINUTES
MAKES: 1 BANANA SPLIT

1   banana, unpeeled
1   T peanut butter
15   chocolate chips

1. Create a pocket in the banana by slicing it lengthwise down to the bottom peel, but not through it.
2. Fill the slot with peanut butter and chocolate chips. Wrap the banana in aluminum foil and toss in the campfire embers.
3. Cook until peanut butter and chocolate chips have melted, about 5 minutes. Carefully remove from the fire and cool slightly before eating.

S'more Fun
Around
the
Campfire

Grab some of my
gelatin-free
ChillOver Powder
and whip up a batch of
homemade marshmallows.

(order online at MaryJanesFarm.org)

Here, I'll show you how ...

MaryJane's Marshmallows

PREP TIME: 30 MINUTES
COOK TIME: 25 MINUTES
MAKES: 36 MARSHMALLOWS

9   t MaryJane's ChillOver Powder (3 boxes or buy in bulk, p. 179)
1¼ cups water, divided
2½ cups sugar
1   cup light corn syrup
½   t salt
2   T vanilla extract
2   egg whites
¼   t cream of tartar
powdered sugar for dusting

1. In a small saucepan, sprinkle ChillOver Powder into ¾ cup cold water. Place over medium-low heat and stir constantly, using a whisk, for only 3 minutes. Set aside. The consistency will be that of a thick paste.
2. In a 3-quart saucepan, blend together ½ cup water with the sugar, corn syrup, and salt. Bring to a slow boil.
3. Turn heat to medium high. Continue to cook, unstirred, until a candy thermometer inserted into the mixture reaches 240°F. (Do not overcook, or your marshmallows will be tough.) Remove from heat. Pour in ChillOver paste and whisk until dissolved. Stir in vanilla.
4. In the bowl of a large mixer, beat the egg whites until frothy and add cream of tartar. Beat until soft peaks form. Using a low speed, pour hot syrup slowly into beaten egg mixture. After all the syrup is added, increase to high speed and continue to beat for 15 minutes.
5. Spread the mixture into an 8"-square pan that has been heavily dusted with powdered sugar. Dust top. Let dry uncovered overnight.
6. Loosen the mixture from the pan by lifting around edges with a knife.
7. Turn out onto a powdered-sugar-dusted cutting board.
8. Dust bottom again with powdered sugar, using a handheld sifter.
9. Cut into squares with a large knife that has been dusted with powdered sugar. Dust the pieces completely and use for campfire s'mores.

Flavored Marshmallows

Chocolate & Caramel Swirls

¾ cup chocolate chips
¼ cup corn syrup
2 T light brown sugar
3 T butter
⅛ t vanilla

Fold in chocolate chips after Step 4 (left). After spreading the mixture into an 8"-square pan (Step 5), top with caramel sauce (following), allow to dry overnight, then continue with Step 9 (left).

1. In a small saucepan over medium heat, bring corn syrup, sugar, and butter to a boil, stirring frequently. Once the mixture begins to boil, stop stirring and continue to boil until the temperature reaches 240°F on a candy thermometer. Stir in vanilla.
2. Pour caramel into a small pitcher or a funnel with a flow control. Pour the caramel in parallel lines across the marshmallows.
3. Run a wooden skewer or sharp knife across the lines of caramel, alternating directions after each pass through.

Pretzel & Pineapple

¾ cup crushed pretzels
½ cup chopped dried pineapple

Fold in ingredients after Step 4 (left).

Chocolate Crumb & Peanut Butter

1 cup crushed chocolate cookie crumbs
½ cup peanut butter
¾ cup peanuts, chopped

Fold in cookie crumbs and peanut butter after Step 4 (left). After Step 9, top marshmallows with chopped peanuts.

Entertainment

You're OUT THERE, honey ...

Out on the highway, cruising the countryside. You might be crooning "Trailer for sale or rent ..." at the top of your lungs. Why not? You're Queen of the Road. With gear, gumption, and glam to burn, there's nothing to stop you now. But slow down a minute, sister. There's no need to hightail it to the horizon while the world outside your window passes in a blur. Getting there is half the fun.

What you need is a go-to to-do list, brimming with marvelous mini-excursions to make your getaway even more exciting. Pick one of your passions, or whip up a wish list of things you never have enough time to do at home. With a smidgen of research, you can put together a glamperific travel guide perfectly tailored to your wandering whims. Are you ready?

I'm about to rev up your engine ...

I BRAKE FOR
JUNK

IN THIS CHAPTER

Destination: Learncation

yoga cowgirls (top) and filmstrip photo #5 courtesy of Jennifer Denison | filmstrip photos #1,3,4 courtesy of Suzanne Cummings

Consider cruising to a destination where you can pick up skills you've always wanted to learn.

You'll get all the benefits of being away from work, bills, and housecleaning. Plus, you'll gain a deep sense of fulfillment that comes from broadening your horizons.

Many modern adventurers are putting an academic spin on the traditional vacation concept and loving their "learncations" even more.

Find free resources for travel opportunities that incorporate education, wellness, crafting, culture, and more on these sites: ShawGuides.com and RealAdventures.com.

Are you a "Reel" Woman?

Imagine this: Cool water flowing along a rocky stream bed invites you toward the pebbled bank. You drop your gear and start preparing your line. When the hook is baited, you cast gracefully upstream and watch the line float down just short of the tangle where you know the fish are gathered. Time to wade out into the water. You squeal when the chill hits your ankles but push on until it reaches the cuff of your shorts. This is the stuff "tough" is made of. Yep, you're a "reel" woman.

 ## You Get a Line, I'll Get a Pole ...

If you've ever had the urge to fish, there's no better time than now. After all, you're on the loose!

- Women of all backgrounds and experience levels are wading into the water to satisfy their wildest urges. There are over 17 million female anglers in the U.S. who are passionately reclaiming their right to America's last sacred sport.
- Unfamiliar with the territory? You'll find lots of helping hands to guide you on your journey. From bait, flies, and old-timer tips to fillets in the frying pan, you'll find the know-how you'll need to start.

Sisters on the Fly

is a growing group of women who caravan around the country in cute vintage trailers, fishing, running rivers, and having "more fun than anyone." They'll show you the ropes and spoil you rotten. Learn more at SistersOnTheFly.com.

Loyal Order of the Glamper ("'Tis better to glamp than camp.")

is based online and they occasionally meet up here and there in smaller groups. No fees to join, no rally dues. Online conversations contain a wealth of information, everything from how to paint your barbeque grill pink to trailer renovations to trailers for sale. Learn more at LoyalOrderOfTheGlamper.com.

Farmgirls on the Loose

was started by women who are dues-paying members of MaryJane's Farmgirl Sisterhood, now numbering 4,000 plus. Learn more at FarmgirlsOnTheLoose.org.

Feeling Sporty?

If outdoor sporting is your game, the world is your oyster.

Whether it's a restful yoga retreat you relish or a wet-'n'-wild rafting adventure,
here are starting points for embarking on your sporty sabbatical:

Trails.com

- Easy day hikes, tough treks, biking trails, and extended overnight backpacking trips throughout North America
- In-depth access to trail maps, driving directions, and detailed descriptions of routes
- Links to USGS topographic maps as well as photos, trail elevation profiles, regional locator maps, and interesting facts about the natural, geographical, and historical significance of various hikes and regions

Oars.com

- Top-notch guide service for river and coastline rafting trips worldwide
- More trip options than any other North American whitewater rafting company
- Trips tailored to your experience level and limited to small groups, maintaining the best guide-to-guest ratio in the business

YogaFinder.com

- Online directory of yoga retreats, instructors, and facilities worldwide

HorseRentals.com

- Straightforward list of stables by state with contact information and a brief description of services for each listing

HomeRanch.com

- Women's Yoga and Horsemanship Retreats

Go Geocaching

This fun-for-all-ages game puts an exciting new spin on traditional scavenger-hunt expeditions.

It can be played just about anywhere, and since players can also log on to a website to record their findings, the game offers the added thrill of connecting outdoor adventurers around the globe.

- Geocache locations range from city parks to mountaintops, so you're likely to find one (or more) along the way.
- Search for sites and learn more about the game at Geocaching.com.

Junktiquing

What woman doesn't love to go junktiquing?

If you're an impassioned picker of eclectic "junk" (affectionate term for antiques, collectibles, and can't-live-without kitschy knick-knacks), a road trip is a fabulous excuse for a junking jaunt.

Of course, a seasoned picker can track down splendid, spontaneous treasures as she travels, but why not pinpoint a few intriguing destinations before you set sail? Mark hot spots on your map using these websites: AntiquesNavigator.com and FindAFleaMarket.com.

Glamping Getaways

Choosing a 5-Star Glamping Experience

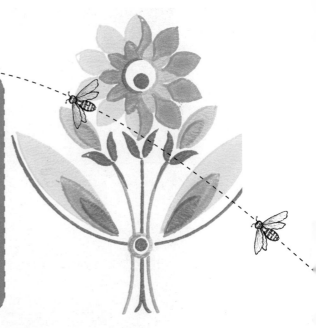

Websites like Glamping Girl (GlampingGirl.com) are available to help you choose your destination.

GlampingGirl.com is your personal guide to luxury camping and glamping. Find out about the newest and hottest gadgets and gear. Search the directory for a glamping resort or luxury campground near you or around the world. GlampingGirl.com will make sure you enjoy the great outdoors without roughing it. No matter what your budget is, there is a glamping option for you.

Kirurumu,
Tanzania
Kirurumu.net

" Regardless of budget, you can enjoy the great outdoors without sacrificing luxury. "

– GlampingGirl.com

Cariad Canvas
Pembrokeshire, England
CariadCanvas.co.uk

MaryJanesFarm B&B,
Idaho
MaryJanesFarm.org/bb

Also, check out international sites!
Where?

Storm Creek Outfitters,
Idaho
StormCreekOutfitters.com

The easiest way to keep up on the latest news and updates
about glamping events and getaways?

InternationalGlampingWeekend.com

Glamping doesn't have to happen away from home. If you have a back yard, a rooftop, a porch, a deck, or a small patch of grass under a cool shady tree, you can have a glamping spot all your own. It's easy! Decorate your deck with pretty accents. Plump up some soft, white pillows and sleep under the stars. Adorn that old picnic table with a handful of candles and a pitcher overflowing with your favorite flowers. Selecting a bit of personalized glam and hauling it out your back door is what glamping is all about. When a woman gets that glamping look in her eye, nothing in her immediate outside world is ever the same.

"My glamping checklist includes a vintage picnic basket that has real china and real silverware in it, along with cloth napkins, tea towels, dishcloths, some cooking utensils, etc. And YES, there are china teacups with saucers in there."
– CJ, Colorado

"How wonderful that you and your grown daughter are able to break away to go glamping. I love all the fanciness you did. I would love to do that, but I have a hubby who would never put up with that much girly stuff. But LOOK OUT once I get a canopy up in my yard!!!!"
        – Janet, Michigan

"Thanks, Janet. We don't do it that way when our husbands are camping with us. We tell them we are going "glamping" and they KNOW it's girl camping and there will be girly stuff galore. If our husbands come, it's a whole different *animal.*"
        – CJ and Robin

Glamper Wisdom

When smoking a fish, never inhale.

If you value your privacy, place a tuba outside your glamper.

Glamping Gatherings

My girlfriends are the sisters
I picked out for myself.

> For there is no friend like a sister, in calm or stormy weather, to cheer one on the tedious way, to fetch one if one goes astray, to lift one if one totters down, to strengthen whilst one stands.
> – Christina Rossetti

Gather up, girlfriends!

trailers photo (top) courtesy of Suzanne Cummings

Chai Green Tea

10 Tips for the Girl Camping Hostess

(from Girl-Camping.blogspot.com)

Are you ready to share your yen for camping by staging a gathering for fellow girl campers? If so, we salute you—because someone has to be the hostess if there are going to be camping parties for others to enjoy!

These are some tips you might find helpful as you make your mostest-hostess plans:

1. Let your guests know what to expect/what to bring.
Examples: Are pets OK? Are meals provided, or are you planning for potluck contributions? Are water and power available, or is this a dry-camping event? Will your guests need any special clothing or gear—swimsuit, party outfit, fishing gear, etc.? Should they bring firewood? Will they need money for meals out, special entertainment, campsite fees, shopping?

2. Provide a GPS address in addition to written directions.
It's now very common for drivers to use a GPS rather than written directions, and we understand why, especially when towing a trailer. It's not always easy to turn a trailer around if you take a wrong turn, nor to read from a sheet of paper while doing the driving. You will have happier guests if they don't have to "undo" being lost in the effort of trying to find you.

3. Post signage at the last couple of intersections.
Put yourself in a first-timer's shoes—even with a GPS, it's always nice to know that you're going the right way as you get close to an event site.

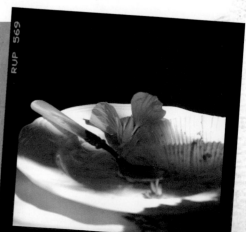

4. Be ready to help with parking.
Many gals are rookies at parking a trailer, and even the more experienced ones will appreciate having a spotter as they do their maneuvering into a parking spot.

5. Provide a nametag for every guest.
These can be as simple or as creatively elaborate as you wish. They're important, in any case, because they help to break the social ice and make it easy for everyone to learn and remember names. (Of course, if you're only inviting those who know each other already, this step isn't so important.)

6. Create a central gathering spot and mark it.
Everyone likes to know where they can go for questions, meals, departures for activities, and so forth. We love using a large, stand-up chalkboard for this purpose—messages and memos can easily be changed—but do whatever works for you.

7. Make the first night's meal flexible and easy.
Chances are, your guests will be trickling in over a span of time (some will arrive late if they've had to work that day), and that they'll also be consumed by getting set up once they do arrive. A hot-dog roast is a good way to go, with or without some crockpot dishes that don't have to be served at a specific time. If the first night will be an "on your own" meal night, be sure to let everyone know that ahead of time.

8. Set a time for trailer-touring.
Every girl camper we've ever met just loves to show off her trailer and all its goodies to her fellow campers (if not to the general public). But let's face it—when you're camping in a trailer, it's not always as tidy as you'd like, and it takes a little time to glam it back up. So it's just nice for your guests to know when they can expect to have camera-toting company!

GIRL CAMP, USA
Girl-Camping.blogspot.com

9. Take good care of your new gals.
Think back to the first time you took your camping rig somewhere public, and/or the first time you camped with women you didn't know. Were you uncertain? Shy? Scared you wouldn't fit in? Worried that you didn't have everything "perfect"? Afraid to ask any questions? This will help you remember to pay extra attention to those who are new and to keep them under that welcoming wing.

10. Prepare for the unexpected.
It's always a good idea to keep a first-aid kit handy, and to keep an ICE (In Case of Emergency) number for every guest. Emergency-room addresses/directions can come in handy, too. As careful as we all try to be, accidents and injuries can and do sometimes happen, and as hostess, you'll be the ipso-facto person in charge.

Now—add in your own special planning, get those invitations out, and get ready for an awesome time!

Where to Go

National Parks, etc.

Boondocks [boon-doks]

Butters family gypsy camp, 1950s

As in, "I hitched up my vintage trailer and headed out to the boondocks to escape the hubbub of the city."

But, wait—there's a new twist on the term that hasn't hit the dictionaries (yet). Want to try it? Repeat after me:

"Come on, girls, let's round up the wagons and go *boondocking* this weekend!"

Yep, boondocking.

It means camping in remote, rural, or provincial areas. Off the beaten paths of conventional campgrounds. Off the grid. Toss "boondocking" out in a conversation with seasoned trailer travelers, and some will be savvy.

"All the cool campers do it," they'll say.

Boondocking can also be referred to (in tamer terms) as "dispersed camping," which government agencies like the U.S. Forest Service deem "camping outside developed campgrounds."

The gist is this: boondocking offers a bit more rugged camping experience, but it's footloose—and free.

Pros:
- no fees to pay
- gorgeous campsite possibilities
- privacy (no neighbors, no noise)

Cons:
- no hookups or restrooms
- vulnerability away from neighboring campers

Boondocking on private land can be tricky.

Even when visiting friends and family, there may be city or county regulations that prohibit RVs or other trailers from parking on streets (private driveways are fair game). A quick call to the local police station will tell you if street parking is legal.

In rural areas, you may be able to boondock on a private ranch or farm. If you happen upon a great spot and can locate the landowner, it never hurts to ask.

In a pinch, boondocking in a parking lot is a possibility. If you've been driving for hours and need a rest, businesses like WalMart, K-Mart, Costco, and Cracker Barrel, and various grocery stores, churches, and other businesses, may allow overnight parking in their lots. During business hours, you can pop inside and ask permission. Often, these lots are protected by security cameras and guards, making them a safer sleeping option than, say, a dark alley. Again, check with local law enforcement to avoid being ousted in the middle of the night.

Public Land

As a general rule, boondocking is allowed anywhere on federal public lands within 300 feet of any established road, and 200 feet from water sources (creeks, lakes, etc).

Federal Land Administrators:

- U.S. Forest Service (www.FS.Fed.us)
- Bureau of Land Management (BLM.gov)
- Army Corps of Engineers (www.USACE.Army.mil)
- Bureau of Reclamation (www.USBR.gov)
- U.S. Fish and Wildlife Service (www.FWS.gov)

Note: National parks do not allow boondocking.

State agencies may also allow boondocking, but it's best to check with your state's land management agencies to be sure.

Unless an area is restricted from dispersed camping, you can simply stake out a perfect spot and set up camp. Of course, boondockers are encouraged to make minimal impact on the land. The "Leave No Trace" concept is key when you're camping outside designated campgrounds that undergo regular garbage patrols and maintenance. Your best bet is to make use of previously established boondock campsites where you'll find a convenient place to park and an existing campfire ring.

In most boondocking-friendly areas, you can stay 14 continuous days for free, but subsequent camping days must be 25 miles away. Exceptions include Bureau of Land Management Long-term Visitor Areas, which allow stays of several months for a nominal fee.

How to Find Boondocking Sites in Advance

The USA Camping Map at RV-Camping.org has links to each state's public lands administrators' websites—a great place to start looking for boondocking locations.

Arm yourself with good maps such as Benchmark Maps or Atlas & Gazetteers by DeLorme Publishing Company. These maps highlight federal and state lands as well as established campgrounds that can serve as jump-off points for boondockers. Contact local public lands administrators for specific regulations.

For the technologically inclined, a Web application at Boondocking.org allows you to enter GPS coordinates for your favorite camping spots and find other spots near your current location. You can also search for free automobile-accessible camping areas based on a distance from a given latitude and longitude point.

Traditional RV Campgrounds

If boondocking isn't your style (and who doesn't love running water and electricity once in a while?), then there are tons of conventional RV campgrounds that provide parking spots, hookups, restrooms, and other facilities for a fee. Find a site at RV There Yet (RVThereYet.cc).

WiFi

Business on the Road in Your PJs
(you can run, but they will find you)

Let's face it: You can run, hop the fence, hightail it to the horizon—but it will find you.

What's tracking you down?

Work, my friend. The daily grind.

Let me tell you from experience that it's tough to get all the way off the grid, even on vacation.

Work has a way of sniffing you out, and, before you know it, it's hot on your trail.

Unless you're prepared to get die-hard and ditch communication while you're traveling, you'll need a way to stay connected that's simple and reliable, whether you're in an RV park or a remote boondock camp.

The word we're looking for here is "wireless." In techie-talk, it's "WiFi," pronounced why-fie. (We all know why-pie?)

In short, these terms refer to the technology used to make computers and mobile phones work via signals that bounce around "out there" in space. Get the gadgets that suit your style, and you'll have on-the-road access, no physical connections needed.

Even if you're bent on leaving business in the rearview mirror, wireless Internet capabilities can come in handy. You'll love being able to Google, scout out stuff to do, check weather forecasts (check knitting forecasts?), e-mail, and blog about your adventures along the way.

The top three options for wireless Internet while road tripping are:

WiFi hotspots
(available free at certain locations
like airports and coffee shops)

- - - - - - - - - - - -

mobile
(cell phone service networks
based on transmitting towers)

- - - - - - - - - - - -

satellite
(based on satellite signals)

Mobile Basics

Pros:
- works anywhere you get cell-phone reception
- allows mobile Internet access (you can connect while driving)
- costs less than satellite
- download speeds don't fluctuate with weather conditions

Cons:
- without cell reception, you can't connect to the Internet

Equipment You'll Need:
- computer or handheld device
- access to a service provider's network and modem (usually provided by carrier)
- router (optional, for accessing your connection with laptops or handhelds)
- booster antenna (optional, for boosting a weak signal due to your location or your trailer's construction—Airstreams and metal teardrops, take note)

When shopping for a service provider (also called a carrier), ask about:
- coverage where you might be traveling (some providers offer greater areas of cell signals than others)
- bandwidth (speed) and the amount of data allowed based on their service plan (to stream media or download large files, you may need more of both)
- cost and contract terms

Service Providers:
- VerizonWireless.com (so far, the best for rural coverage)
- Sprint.com
- ATT.com (AT&T)

Satellite Made Simple

Pros:

- works anywhere, no matter how remote

Cons:

- costs more than mobile (system and installation costs plus monthly service)
- only allows stationary Internet access (you can't connect while driving)
- download speeds can lag during inclement weather
- satellite dish requires a clear "line of sight" to the sky
- usually slower than mobile

Equipment You'll Need:

- computer or handheld device
- satellite dish and modem (usually provided by carrier)
- mounting bracket (for auto-point systems)
- tripod, GPS, and compass (for manual-point systems)

An auto-point satellite system is, as the name implies, fully automatic. The dish is mounted to the outside of your trailer, and when you come to a stop, it rotates to find the best signal. This option will pinch your pocketbook, with system and installation costs soaring up into the $5,000 to $7,000 range, and there are monthly service fees to boot.

Auto-Point Installation Companies:
- Motosat.com
- GroundControl.com
- Starband.com

A manual-point system is cheaper ($1,000 to $2,500 to install), but it's not as easy to use. Hands-on manipulation is necessary each time you want to connect to the Internet. You have to set up a tripod, determine your location via GPS, point your dish with the aid of a compass, and so on. Then there's the fine print: mobility (dish transport) is not officially approved by installation companies, so you can't call for help with pointing the dish properly.

Manual-Point Installation Companies:
- Hughes.com
- BroadBandToGo.com

Traveling with Fidos & Kiddos

It isn't beware of dog, it's BEWARE!—kids and pets on board.

A dog harness keeps Fido secure and protects drivers and passengers. Kurgo.com

I'm intent on instilling a love of glamping in my grandgirls, so we schedule what they call "Nanny night." Dogs and children allowed. Also allowed? ...

Campfire dinners, costume jewelry (Nanny brings plenty to choose from), outdoor bathing, late-night storytelling, sleeping-bag toe tickling, treasure hunts, and TEA. I've conditioned my grandgirls to stop for tea with me to sip what I call a London Fog—white tea with milk (fresh from my cow). The tea part of glamping with kiddos gives *me* a much-needed pause because the one bit of solid, irrefutable advice I have about glamping with kids is this: Make them the center of your attention, pretty much the only thing you're doing (the reason you'll need scheduled tea breaks). If kids are an add-on or an aside when you venture outside, everyone ends up frustrated because kids are so ravenously curious about every detail nature has to offer. Plus, they're without their usual technological distractions—you're it!

And our doggie poohs? Ruffing it with dogs comes down to one simple rule—leave only paw prints (you know what I'm talking about). The Sisters on the Fly (p. 186) are fond of saying, "We have no rules except one: No husbands, kids, or dogs." Can you imagine the glamping sister who pulls her trailer to an event and her dog barks all night or overturns the first night's potluck table? Never a good thing. Traveling can be stressful for dogs. In other words, don't expect your dog to spend the day in a car, get into camp, and settle down for the night. Allocate time to walk and play with your dog. Rules regarding dogs and campgrounds are becoming increasingly strict, for good reason. Consider enrolling your dog in the AKC's Canine Good Citizen program. Public campgrounds that frown on dogs are more likely to welcome your dog if you can show them your dog is certified well-behaved.

Glamping with Nanny

The first thing a glamping gal does is find flowers for her hair and the dinner table.

I scout around and find firewood so Nanny can get our campfire started.

Then I help with preparing the outside bath. I use a garden hose to fill the tub with cold water, and Nanny lights a propane burner beneath it. After dinner and s'mores, the water will be perfect and we'll take a bath under the stars.

To the gardens we go for potatoes, garlic, shallots, carrots, and basil. I stop at the henhouse to gather eggs for breakfast. Nothing but organic for our hobo dinner! I LOVE eating bell peppers as if they're apples.

Nanny puts our hobo dinners (p. 177) right in the campfire to cook and I set the table for dinner.

Now on to dessert! This glamper makes s'mores using Nanny's homemade marshmallows (p. 180). You haven't tasted marshmallows until you've tasted REAL marshmallows like ours toasted over a campfire, rolled in mini chocolate chips, and smooshed between two graham crackers. Oh my!

International Glamping Weekend

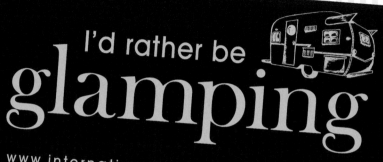

I'd rather be glamping

www.internationalglampingweekend.com

When I came up with the idea for an international glamping celebration, I was trying to accomplish two things. First, I knew glampers would love the idea of a designated weekend dedicated to outdoor fun. Second, I felt like the glamping trend was catching on big-time (glamping this and glamping that showing up everywhere here and there), but the glamping movement was in need of only ONE website, one hub, where we could find an all-inclusive list of glamping websites or blogs, in addition to a current "glamping in the news" section, as well as a complete run-down of glamping gatherings.

Thinking about buying a trailer? Remodeling the one you have and need help with what propane fridge to buy? Looking for some decorating ideas?

International Glamping Weekend is it, glampers! It's THE hub, THE happenin' place for all things glamping.

220

INTERNATIONAL
glamping
WEEKEND™

Brought to you by
MARYJANESFARM®

June 1–2, 2013

a weekend dedicated to glamorous camping

list your
glamping
gathering

Not all
who wander
are lost!

With news giants like *The New York Times*, *Wall Street Journal*, *The Today Show*, and *CNN* finally giving glampers their due, it's high time for an official, designated glamping weekend. And who else to decree it but the woman (moi) who pioneered the concept?

Fire up your dream machine! There is a glamping round-up every year the first weekend in June, anywhere in the world (back yards, rooftops, and city parks notwithstanding). Dust off your prom dress, pack up your mule, load up on chocolate, and gather up your glamping gal friends. This is the website where, finally, all of us glamper types are showing up on the same page. If I've missed your website or blog, give a hoot, give a holler, I'm all yours. And if you have ideas for other ways I can honor and showcase what we're about, I'm all ears.

In sisterhood,

MaryJane ♡

glamping@maryjanesfarm.org

Get your FREE bumper sticker!

Send a self-addressed, stamped #10 envelope to:
GLAMPING
BOX 8691
Moscow, ID 83843
(limit one per address)

When in doubt, go glamping!

Add this to your website.

Glamping in the News

• Luxury Camping for Comfort Queens – 7 Top Glamping Destinations (featuring MaryJanesFarm), Wicked Good Travel Tips, April 2012

• Glamping in Idaho (featuring MaryJanesFarm), Glamping Girl, March 2012

• 20 Decadent Glamping Photos (featuring MaryJanesFarm), BuzzFeed, March 2012

• Glamping It Up, Irish Times, March 2012

• Australia's Most Glamorous Camping Destinations, Huffington Post, February 2012

• Glamping, Florida Style, VisitFlorida.com, February 2012

• Glamping Hub Puts High-end Camping on the Map, Travel Daily News, February 2012

• 'Glamping' Will Let You Experience the Great Outdoors with Creature Comforts, TheLedger.com, February 2012

• Glamping: Where Nature Meets Luxury, Yahoo! Finance, December 2011

• A Guide to "Glamping" Around the World, Condé Nast Traveler, December 2011

• Pioneer of "Glamping" Helps Americans Unplug and Stay Healthy (featuring MaryJanesFarm), Black Enterprise, Boston Globe, Charlotte Observer, Cincinnati Enquirer, Columbus Dispatch, FinanzNachrichten.de, Houston Chronicle, Market Watch, Miami Herald, Morning Star, NY Daily News, San Jose Mercury News, SFGate.com, Synacor, Yahoo! Finance, December 2011

(and more!)

Glamping Websites & Blogs

• Adeeni Design Blog—Luxury Camping: I am definitely a glamper, not a camper

• Alison Travels

• A Little Campy

• Bargain Hoot—Glamping: glamorous camping!

• Becoming an Outdoors Woman

• Brown Folk Festival—How to Go 'Glamping'—That's Glamorous Camping

• Camp and RV Cook

• Camping in Heels

• Camping in Montana

• Camping Road Trip

• Camping USA

• Camping Women

• The Everyday Gourmet food blog

• Farm Stay U.S.

• Flickr Glamping Group

• Giddy Up 4 Branson

• Ginger Goes Glamping

(and more!)

What do you get when you toss eight farmhands into a pressure cooker, turn the heat up for three months until it whistles, add friends until blended, fold in family, combine with a publisher, then cover with two cameras?

Acknowledgments

To whip up pages, Alicia Baker, Carol Hill, Patti Fulton, Sandi Day, Jennifer Bové, and Gabe Gibler bubbled in front of their computers; Alicia Carlson sprinkled in plenty of food photos; Suzanne Cummings offered Sisters on the Fly glamping photos; Farmgirl Sisters Shery Jespersen and Michele Heib stirred in a dab of crafting and Sisters CJ Armstrong and Melanie Gilmore added a pinch of playful; Mig Whitt and Juli Thorson added cute trailers to the mix; Alyson Oüten and Gibbs Smith showed up for a glampout; editor Suzanne Taylor suggested the recipe; former employees Cindylou Ament and Heather McCoy (and husband John Saltarella) added flair; Rochelle Smith brought her knitting needles; Julie Tibbets added awesome!; Kim Jones kept my cows milked while I took photos; Brian Westgate drilled and hammered; daughter Megan Rae edited, crafted, posed, and posited; daughter-in-law Ashley Ogle blended the entire food section (round of applause); Priscilla Wegars proofed; son-in-law Lucas Rae kept things from boiling over (paid the bills); son Brian Ogle offered up his usual over-the-top customer service; and husband Nick Ogle, my gaffer and key grip, kept my goose from getting cooked. Makes about 224 pages. Best served with love and buttered buns.

Index

Where complexions
are fine ...

THERE IS ALWAYS PINE!

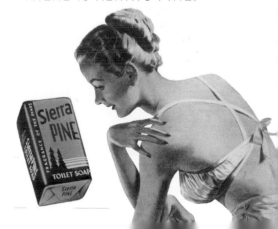

About the author ...

With an impressive string of female firsts, MaryJane Butters has always been a pioneer. After graduating from high school in 1971, she was the first woman to attend the Skills Center North Trade School in Ogden, Utah, in carpentry. With a certificate of proficiency in hand, she was hired to build houses at the nearby Hill Air Force Base—the only woman on the crew. From there, she spent her summers watching for fires from a mountaintop lookout in northern Idaho; worked in the Uinta Mountains as one of the first women wilderness rangers in the United States; and in 1976, became the first female station guard at the Moose Creek Ranger Station, the most remote Forest Service district in the continental U.S., in the heart of Idaho's Selway-Bitterroot Wilderness Area. She also built fences in the Tetons of Wyoming, herded cows on the Snake River below Hells Canyon, and raised an organic market garden in White Bird, Idaho.

After moving to her Moscow, Idaho, farm in 1986, she founded a regional environmental group still thriving today (PCEI.org). After four years, she resigned as its director to develop new products for locally grown organic beans that would provide a secure market for farmers transitioning to sustainable production. Along the way, she married her neighbor, Nick Ogle, whose farm borders hers on two sides. Since then, her unique agricultural enterprise has been featured in nearly every major magazine in the country, and in 2008, she was awarded the prestigious Cecil D. Andrus Leadership Award for Sustainability and Conservation. She also sponsors an organic farm apprentice program called Pay Dirt Farm School and runs a wall tent B&B. Her "everyday organic" lifestyle magazine she launched in 2001, *MaryJanesFarm*, is available nationwide and she is the author of four books, with two more in the making. She designs her own line of bedding and home décor sold in 800 department stores, as well as fabric collections.

From her farm, she sells 60 different organic prepared foods and shares the message of simple organic living with readers of her magazine and websites (MaryJanesFarm.org and RaisingJane.org). In addition, she is the creator of Project F.A.R.M. (First-class American Rural Made), an organization that employs rural women who sew totes, quilts, dolls, and more. She is also the owner of the historic Barron Flour Mill in Oakesdale, Washington, and owns two retail stores, one in Coeur d'Alene, Idaho, and one in her hometown of Moscow, Idaho. "Nanny" to half a dozen grandchildren, MaryJane likes to brag that "going granny" has been her most important accomplishment to date. Two of her grown children and their spouses are employed full-time at her farm.

About glamping with girlfriends ...

What woman living in a male-dominated world doesn't need a good, old-fashioned, women-only revival every now and then? Some might call it a support group, but my dues-paying sisterhood organization with more than 4,000 members is a lifeline. Upending long-held notions about a woman's place in the world has been my life's work, not only in the male-dominated field of construction, but also in agriculture. Beginning at age 17, when serving as a student body officer, I took on the state of Utah simply because I thought it might come in handy to be able to wear pants to school every now and then, especially in the dead of winter. Once I rallied the other girls in my school, it was only a matter of time. The year after I graduated, our hard work paid off—girls throughout Utah were given permission to wear pants to school. The work of making the world a better place gets a whole lot easier when you lock elbows with a girlfriend, fuel your body properly, and come to the truly contrary realization that being happy is ultimately more important than being right. My motto: remain playful, no matter the struggle, whatever the outcome. "Give us liberty or give us ... root beer floats and popcorn."

MaryJane ♥

Junktiquing with girlfriends has its rewards!